PERMISSION

TO DO LIFE & BUSINESS YOUR WAY

SARAH STONE

JANE BAKER

authors

AND CO.

CONTENTS

Foreword   v

Introduction   viii

1. Amanda Coles   1
Permission to Empower Yourself

About the Author   28

2. Anna Fairs   30
Permission To Shake Your Tail Feathers

About the Author   55

3. Ashley Cahill   57
Permission to Play to your strengths

About the Author   77

4. Beverley Fray   80
Permission to break the cycle of settling, do yourself
JUSTICE

About the Author   100

5. Brenda Gabriel   102
Permission to be a reality star (Even if you have no
desire to be on TV)

About the Author   133

6. Deasha Waddup   136
Permission to get outside your comfort zone and grow
your business organically.

About the Author   156

7. Helen Jane   158
Permission to Throw Away the Rule Book.

About the Author   186

8. Jo Gilbert   189
Permission to Live Life Your Way

About the Author   209

9. Nadine de Zoeten   211
   Permission to Rest and Receive

   About the Author   235
10. Nicole Thorne   238
   Permission to exercise your way!

   About the Author   258
11. Sera Johnston   260
   Permission to be You – Unlock the Person Within.

   About the Author   287
12. Simon Kozlowski   289
   Permission to rise to Rockstar status

   About the Author   325
   Personal Note Of Congratulations   327
   Sarah Stone   329
   Jane Baker   332

FOREWORD

ANDREA MCLEAN

When I quit my job live on TV in November 2020, a number of things happened.

Firstly, I cried, which took me by surprise because quitting was something I'd wanted to do for a while, and I didn't expect to be blubbing on the telly.

Secondly, the world became split in two; between those who thought I was brave to walk away from a high-profile, well-paid job to follow my dreams. And those who thought I was mad.

Interestingly, the ones who thought I was mad were those who worked in my industry, because no one EVER walks away from a job on the telly, unless they've got a bigger or better job on the telly... I just had an online business and a dream of helping millions of women around the world think differently about themselves and the life they're living. The ones who thought I was brave were the women (and men) who contacted me to say they *wished* they could walk away from a job that they were unhappy in, that they felt stuck but too scared to do anything about it.

It didn't occur to me that it was brave. It was just something I HAD to do. After 25 years working as a TV presenter I'd done all kinds of amazing things, and interviewed all kinds of amazing people - from Oprah Winfrey to Love Island reality stars and everyone in between. I loved telly, but it didn't light my fire anymore. So I made my list of pros and cons, which became my blueprints for success and blueprints for failure. When I felt like I had covered every possible outcome and was ready to jump - I jumped.

I still spend my days interviewing all kinds of amazing people - but now it's on MY TERMS. We talk about things that excite and ignite us both; personal growth, transformation, aha-moments and so much more! I may not be *seen* by millions of people every day, but I know that I am working towards *improving* the lives of millions - something that means so much more to me than simply being famous.

Each one of the amazing ladies and gentlemen in this book has their own story to tell about leaping into their faith, jumping into the unknown, finding their true calling, and working on themselves until they found their purpose. Each story is unique, just as mine is, and each one will give you own personal aha-moment too. Jump in, soak up their words and let them inspire you.

Give yourself the permission to Think Differently about yourself, your life and your future. How you choose to live it is all in your head, and in your hands.

Andrea McLean.

CEO and Co-Founder www.thisgirlisonfire.com

#1 Sunday Times Best Selling Author

INTRODUCTION

You weren't meant to fit into a box, not in your life or in your business. But it can feel like the opposite especially in the business space.

Everyone seems to have the best way for things to be done, the only way to get the success you desire is to follow this one path. Sometimes it can feel like an echo chamber of all the things you're supposed to be doing and if you don't do it you're destined to not live a life you love, reach the success you desire or just generally reach your goals.

We know because we've seen it, we've experienced it ourselves. In some ways we're some of the lucky ones, we did things our way even if no one else really understood, believed or thought it was the way it should be done.

When we came together towards the end of 2020 and decided to run the "Sell Your Way™" experience we knew we were throwing the doors open to something powerful.

Something that was going to help people find their way to sell, to do business and to ultimately live the life they desired with the success they desired. Giving the permission to do it their way, we've been involved in some amazing things over the years but nothing more powerful than this experience.

Ultimately, that's what business and life should feel like a mind blowing experience, one that you actually enjoy and that includes in your business. Do you ever really create a life you truly love and enjoy if how you do business isn't in a way that lights you up too?

In our opinion, no. We've built businesses and done things other peoples way and to the outside we were successful and our life looked it to. Yet on the inside we felt anything but successful, we didn't enjoy what we were doing or how we were doing it and no matter how amazing other areas of our life were it wasn't that mind blowing experience whilst we felt like a round peg in a square hole when it came to business.

And so we gave ourselves permission to do things our way, to blaze our own paths towards success, business and in life. Instead of following others "must do" strategies we followed what felt right for us, we followed what flowed and came naturally to us.

We shifted how we chose to see things, we shifted how we chose to make decisions, we shifted everything into total alignment with who we are and what lit us up.

The result? A limitless life and business where we live and breathe what we love in all areas on a daily basis. But more than that we're able to trust ourselves, trust our gut, make sales with ease, create in total flow and so much more.

It all started when we gave ourselves permission, and this is what this collaboration book is all about.

At the beginning of the Sell Your Way™ experience we gave each of these authors permission to start doing things their way, permission to explore who they were, what they wanted and how they really wanted to do it.

We gave them permission to throw away the rulebook that they felt they had to follow.

- Permission to throw away the outdated selling strategies and forge their own new relationship with selling and making sales.
- Permission to know what was right for them and trust themselves in following it.
- Permission to do business and life their way.

Now they come together to give YOU permission.

Whether you're feeling stuck in a career that isn't lighting you up, stuck trying to build your business in a way that feels so hard or stuck in fear of showing up as your true self, inside this book you'll find your own permission to rise up and do things your way.

It's time to start a new revolution, not one that has you following someone else's path, but one that has you following yourself, doing it all YOUR WAY!

Ultimately that's our wish for all of you, that you get to build a business and life that is in true alignment with who you are and what truly lights you up.

Our wish is that you discover your way and blaze your own path towards your success. That wish starts here with this book.

www.sellyourwaywithus.com

AMANDA COLES

PERMISSION TO EMPOWER YOURSELF

oday, I am a speaker, trainer, Transformational Empowerment Coach, Clinical Hypnotherapist and NLP Master; a wife and mother of two gorgeous young women.

And what about you, reading this now?

Are you really doing something you love? Are you connected to your bigger purpose in life?

Or are you coasting, doing what you've always done, hoping for a different end result?

Because that was me, for many years. Doing what I'd always done, yet secretly hoping for a different result. Spoiler alert, it never happened.

What if I told you that being human; accepting that you are fallible and vulnerable can actually be a huge strength and propel you to even greater success?

What might happen if you gave yourself permission to believe that that you are not Superwoman? More importantly, what if you realise that you don't need to be and you can be YOU, just the way you are, and still create something extraordinary in your life?

Let me tell you what happened when I accepted all of these points and more. When I truly connected to myself and started to believe that I was worthy of self-love and self-respect, and I had the confidence to act like my life depended on it. Because the truth is, it does.

Above all, what happened when I decided to go all-in and allow the magic to happen, and how a girl who left school at 16, with little formal qualifications and the lofty ambition to become a secretary, ended up as a successful business owner and Executive Coach.

I spent over 20 years as a Leader in People Management; and I've also spent nearly a decade as a Transformational Empowerment Coach, Clinical Hypnotherapist and NLP Master. In my work as a Leader in Corporate, I've coached everyone informally, from C-Suite Executives to shop-floor workers, to prevent burnout and increase their success, and I now bring these unique coaching experiences and perspectives to my business.

These two, very diverse but very inter-connected career choices have given me a unique set of skills and experiences - and a great insight and ability to disrupt and hack the traditional HR model.

In applying scientifically-backed, proven techniques rooted in neuroscience; and using NLP, empathy and positive psychology techniques; I work as a Transformational Empowerment Coach supporting C-Suite Executives, business professionals, corporate leaders, entrepreneurs, and other high-performing clientele. To transform, recalibrate and realign them to magnetically maximise their success in life and business.

This usually translates into eradicating performance issues such as depression, loneliness, fear, anxiety, procrastination; and improving areas such as focus, confidence, goal-setting and achieving, mental preparation, and prevention or recovery from burnout.

Because no matter how successful you are externally, there's generally 'something' that's holding you back from achieving the next level - and it's usually buried in your subconscious; some past unhealed trauma, experienced predominantly as a child or when you were younger.

I am super privileged to be in a position to do what I do and it gives me an enormous sense of satisfaction. But it wasn't always like this and, after over two decades in HR and almost a decade as a Transformational Coach, I've pretty much seen the good, the bad and the ugly of human behaviour.

Today's high achievers need more than just functional expertise. They also need razor-sharp strategy, leadership, risk management and interpersonal skills; a sophisticated skillset, including logistics, marketing, networking strategies, organisational skills and many other talents. All of which are mentally demanding and equally draining if not managed appropriately.

What was once a merely stressful occupation is now becoming unbearable. Business Owners and Leaders are unable to cope with increasing demands. They are becoming more and more burned-out because there is more and more pressure put upon them by others and, more importantly, by themselves

The leaders of today demand and expect much of themselves. These self-imposed expectations are often unsustainable, leading to mental and physical health problems, sleep disorders, addictive behaviour, stress and depression.

After more than 20 years working in organisations and with a thriving private therapy practice, I've seen first-hand the effects that not healing past wounds, working too hard and putting too much pressure on yourself can bring. I've experienced it first hand and I've seen it in my clients and colleagues. Those at 'the coal face' of their business.

I'm here to tell you that not only is it ok to heal yourself from your past, it's also a necessity.

Wearing your past wounds like a badge of honour will not help you in your quest for success - material or personal.

When you decide to take control of your past, in order to create your future - your light shines far more brightly.

The things you desire are far EASIER to come by. You give up the struggles, and instead move into FLOW.

When you give yourself permission to heal, but also give yourself that all important permission to take total responsibility for both your past AND your future, you liberate yourself from the shackles that hold you back.

And in order to do this you have to have enough self-love and self-awareness to let go of all the weight of 'expectation' placed upon you by society; to do what's right for you - and nobody else.

Because yes, making a big change in life is scary.

But you know what is even scarier?

Regret.

Let me start my story, by taking you back to 2019.

It's a Saturday evening in late January. It's freezing cold, and dark. I SHOULD be sat at home, bra off, glass of wine in hand, watching something with Ant and Dec on TV with my husband and two daughters, who are 12 and 10. The dog would be sat at my feet and my elderly cat snoozing on my lap. Yes, that's where I should be.

But I'm most definitely not in Kansas anymore Dorothy.

I am, in fact, sat by myself in an open-air hotel restaurant in rural Dar es Salaam, Tanzania - the Indian ocean is quietly lapping just in front of me, warm sand is sifting gently between my bare toes, and I'm watching the African sunset lazily fade just across the sea, before the darkness descends and stars begin to gently twinkle overhead. The temperature is still a balmy 27 degrees, and my winter-pale skin is loving the heat exposure, although I do look ridiculously white in my newly-purchase sundress.

I've brought a shiny new notebook with me and, as I begin to relax, my thoughts begin to wander to my choices in life, my career and what might come next on my journey.

I've worked in HR nearly all of my career, in one form or another, but now I also have a private hypnotherapy practice. During this trip I'm due to deliver two life coaching sessions to the women I'm yet to meet on this trip, on how they can create more freedom and purpose in their life.

I'm wondering how I can combine the two passions of HR and psychotherapy so I can also create freedom and purpose in my life. But for now, I'm content to watch the sun set across the horizon.

I am feeling very tired, because I've been travelling since late last night, but I'm also giddy with excitement about what the next two weeks will bring. It's taken me two international plane journeys, a VERY long wait at Border Control and an hour long tuk-tuk ride just to get here.

"Here" isn't even my final destination. That comes tomorrow, when I will take a very small, single-prop plane for the final leg of my journey to Mafia; a small island about the same size as the Isle of Wight and 100km south of Zanzibar.

Mafia has no real tourist trade, only a handful of hotels and questionable internet connection due to a very poor economy. I'm going to spend two weeks doing conservation work and swimming with the biggest fish in the sea - Whale Sharks.

What on earth takes a slightly podgy, 46-year-old married mother of two, whose only previous solo journeys have been as far as Tenerife, to rural Tanzania - and more importantly, WHY?

Let me tell you how I ended up in this hotel, planning the next stage of my life because I gave myself permission to create the boundaries I needed and how, if I can do it, so can you.

Let me take you back even further. To the 1970's.

I didn't have the traditional start to life in the golden era of 2.2 kids and the nuclear family.

My parents divorced when I was 3 and I was brought up as an only child by my mother.

My mother and I had a difficult relationship from an early age. She didn't cope well with life and imparted her victim-belief philosophy on everyone around her. Emotional outbursts were regular and usually involved her making a threat to take her own life. As I grew up it was usual for me to go into her bedroom at 3am, just to check she was still breathing.

I wasn't physically neglected, but nonetheless, it was emotional abuse and a toxic environment by the skilled narcissist that she is. She is an expert in emotional blackmail and very manipulative in her behaviour.

I didn't go to university, or even do A-Levels.

I left school at 16 with two GCSEs to my name.

My careers advisor told me the best I could possibly hope for was to be a hairdresser or a secretary. As I didn't fancy working Saturdays, a secretary became my career ambition.

It's not that I wasn't bright, because I was. But I was consistently told that it wasn't worth me applying to university because there was no way my father would pay for it. So, I just didn't bother trying at school. After all, if you're not going to go to uni, and your best career hope is to be a hairdresser or a secretary, A-Levels and a Degree aren't really necessary.

By the time I was 18, things had escalated at home. My mother was increasingly desperate to control me and I was becoming increasingly desperate to release myself from the toxic environment. The arguments and threats were becoming more frequent. After one particularly heated exchange, where she told me she wished she'd never been born and hoped to die, I retorted that I also wished the same for me.

How desperately sad for an 18-year-old girl, with the rest of her life in front of her, to be made to feel that she is not worthy of living by the one person who ought to be championing and protecting her.

What little in the way of self-belief, self-esteem and self-worth I may have had, was being crushed beneath the weight of 15 years of emotional abuse.

I left home two months after my 18th birthday to live with a boyfriend I'd met on holiday two years earlier. Looking back now, I'm not even sure I loved him, but it was a good reason to escape the environment that had held me back and tied my already low self-esteem to a mother determined to do everything she could to destroy it.

Unfortunately, although distance quashed the physical influence she had over me, the emotional abuse I'd suffered during my childhood, which resulted in that lack of self-worth, would manifest itself in life events for the next 22 years.

Sadly, the relationship with that boyfriend dissolved shortly after my 21st birthday, and my next relationship became emotionally, physically and mentally abusive. It only ended when I called the police due to stalking and harassment and I left the shared house we lived in without giving a forwarding address.

The abuse I suffered as a child manifested in me not believing I could have the life success that other people seemed to attract so easily.

I truly believed that everything had to be HARD. It all had to be super difficult, or completely unobtainable.

The only thing I gave myself permission to do, was hate myself and blame myself for not being a braver, better person. I felt disconnected, disjointed in my life and I had no boundaries.

Internally, I suffered with panic attacks, anxiety and sleep problems.

Outwardly at least though, I was doing ok. Opportunities presented themselves to me at work; and I did take advantage of them, working hard to advance my career despite my lack of formal qualifications.

By 23, I was a PA to the Export Director of a large manufacturing firm. He was old school, and liked the 'idea' of a PA more than he actually needed one. So, after three weeks sharpening pencils and photocopying, I approached the HR Manager and asked if there was any other work I could do to keep me busy.

Sure, came the reply, you can be my Administrator. And so, my career in HR was born. The firm sponsored me through a 3-year post-graduate degree and, in 2000, I qualified through a highly-respected Business School.

But this disconnected, disjointed feeling remained. I felt like a fraud inside. The "Imposter Monster" was alive, kicking and living inside my head.

I tried shutting her down. and I tried not listening to her, but the feeling remained - like I was about to be outed any moment as a fraud or a fake; and I'd end up back in front of that school careers officer, who would confidently look me in the eye and say "I told you so".

So instead, I put those feelings in a very secure box in my mind. Once the lid was placed on the box, I wrapped it in metaphorical chains, padlocked it and put it in a dusty cupboard. Much like Pandora's Box, these memories were held securely enough inside the closed box, until it was opened.

I duly kept the box closed, and spent the next 20 years leading people across many diverse disciplines, including telecoms, utilities, leisure and automotive. I worked hard in my career, building up my experience and confidence, only occasionally lifting the lid on the box to shout obscenities at the voice inside telling me I would never achieve anything.

Anyone who has worked in HR for any length of time will tell you the hardest part of the job is dealing with people. And business restructures are the hardest part of dealing with those people. It is never easy, and it never should be. Nobody should ever be happy or make decisions lightly about matters that impact someone's financial ability to care for their family.

I managed my first, large scale redundancy fairly early on in my career and the truth is, that restructure very nearly ended my entire HR career. After making over 90 people redundant, I was then made redundant myself 12 hours later.

I'd like to say I shook it off and bounced back straightaway, but the truth is I opened Pandora's Box and took to my bed for weeks. Burned-out from the experience, I needed time to process it.

I allowed the self-doubt that I had buried come back to the surface. I allowed my feelings of anger, sadness and guilt at losing my job and that of those that I'd also released, to bubble up and it felt awful.

I was hurting badly and I didn't know how to recover. So, I did the only thing I knew how to do. I went on holiday. A week in the sun, with no distractions and no normality was just the tonic I needed to regain a sense of perspective.

I will always attempt to change my physical location, in order to give myself the headspace to make big decisions. I find that physical distance cathartic, head-cleansing and soul-healing. It gives me the ability to see everything more clearly.

When I came back, I threw myself into a new job search and, within two weeks, had secured my next HR role and a hefty salary increase to boot.

That experience did forever change my perspective however, and it shaped my thoughts and actions in subsequent roles. It led me to treat people with the compassion and respect they deserve, and to provide a human-centred approach to Business and Leadership that is all-too-often lacking from organisations more concerned about their profits than their people.

In 2013, I hit a wall.

Pandora's Box was still inside my head; most of the time securely closed, but occasionally it opened itself and unleashed its own version of hell onto my life in the form of panic attacks and increasing episodes of unnecessary anxiety, that occasionally resulted in my own contemplation of the value of my life. I'm not proud of this, but I need to share the power that these thoughts can wield over you in the darkest of times.

The Imposter Monster was also still inside my head, only now she was also giving me parenting AND career advice; and she was sounding more and more like the mother I had walked away from as a broken 18-year-old.

Outwardly successful, but internally falling apart, I was self-aware enough to realise that I needed to do something to change my relationship to the past, otherwise it was going to continue to dictate my future.

My boundaries were failing, and my need to be the perfect wife, the perfect mother and have the perfect career as well was becoming impossible. As it was always destined to. Any self-belief, self-confidence and self-esteem I had was precariously balanced and liable to tip over anytime something even small shook it.

I needed to find out who I really was, find out who I've really been all these years. To reconnect myself to me. To rebuild my sense of self-belief, self-confidence and self-love that had been lost along the way.

The fascination I have with psychology and people, coupled with the prospect of healing my own past, led me to spend a year training to become a Clinical Hypnotherapist, Master NLP Practitioner and Life/Business Coach.

The healing I knew I needed to do, but knowing is very different to doing. Slaying my own personal demons was a vital part of me creating the boundaries I needed to in order to create the life I wanted.

The training was hard: over a year of therapy on myself as much as helping others.

It took all the parts of me I thought were broken, and slowly but surely started to put them back together.

Pandora's Box was opened, shaken, emptied and dusted. Internal, dusty and discarded lightbulbs were changed for bright LED lights that were permanently switched on, and parts of me that I didn't even know existed, were able to shine.

And the most important part was, for the first time in a very long time, I began to give myself permission to reconnect to who I really was and what I really wanted. Instead of being driven by circumstances, I began to feel that I could create circumstances and situations for my own benefit.

Finally, the old wounds from my childhood began to heal and I was, and still am, able to accept that my upbringing wasn't my fault.

I have always been enough, exactly the way I am.

I just wish I'd been able to hear that oh- so-simple phrase - and believe it - 30 years ago.

I am not to blame for the abuse I suffered as a child. But I am responsible for everything I create now.

And living my life through the lens of the child who didn't know any better was no longer a viable option. It was now time to heal those childhood traumas and up-level.

This healing process is like trying a dress on for size from somewhere you've never bought from before.

It feels awkward at first. Fitting in all the wrong places. It's a weird length, the arms feel strange and you're not sure about the neckline.

I toyed with the idea of returning this 'healing dress' because I wasn't sure I was ever going to wear it; but against the odds, I decided to keep it. I kept trying it on periodically. And as I did that, a strange phenomenon occurred.

The more I tried it on, the more I liked it. The more I looked at myself in the mirror wearing it, the more I realised it suited me.

The dress gave me the confidence and the realisation that I could reconnect to who I was and what I wanted, and that was OK.

I still wear that dress today. I put it on every time I start to doubt myself, just to remind me who the hell I really am.

I am proud to be me.

Fast forward a few years to 2019.

I was busy with work, I was busy being a wife, busy being a mother to my two girls, and busy running a business; but I had a sudden urge one dull Wednesday that I needed to travel once more.

The thing was, I wasn't sure where I needed to travel to. But travel is my go-to when I feel the urge to up-level and I had that butterfly feeling in the pit of my tummy.

That feeling that could mean anxiety, or it could mean excitement. I wasn't sure which it was right then, but I knew I was on the cusp of breaking through something huge inside of me, if I could only connect to it.

I knew, intuitively, that it involved me going somewhere out of the ordinary.

This is a strange feeling as I've never done the 'traditional' travelling. I didn't do the gap year, where kids go off to 'find themselves', as I was busy using an old typewriter, working in a dodgy company that imported American cars.

But I do inherently understand the power that travel brings.

I toyed with the idea of a charity trek. You know the ones:

Bike your way across the Inca Trail to Macchu Picchu;

Hike the Great Wall of China;

Ride the Himalayas.

And I loved the idea of them.

But I also appreciated that, inherently, I'm lazy, and they all seemed to involve a great deal of preparation.

Hiking, Biking and Walking all involve training. Lots of training. And I didn't have the time or the inclination for that.

I can't even remember now where I first saw it.

A web page. Advertising a trip to Tanzania. I had to look up where Tanzania was. I'll be honest and say I kept mistaking it for Tasmania. No, Amanda, completely different places.

But this wasn't just any trip. No. This was different.

Spend 10 days swimming with Whale Sharks (that get up to 15m or more in length). Do some conservation work - record their movements for an international database. Beach cleans, yoga, and trips to local schools. Just 10 places and only for women.

THIS. WAS. IT.

SOLD.

I could swim. Admittedly, I'm not the strongest of swimmers, but hey, I can swim 40 lengths of my local municipal pool at a push. And I've been snorkelling in Greece.

How hard could it be to swim in the Indian Ocean whilst watching and recording fish that are 15 metres long?

Granted, I'd never been diving, but the web page was clear - no diving experience was necessary. Snorkelling was fine in order to swim and record the necessary information needed.

The conservation part of the trip was also a huge lure for me. Doing work that would benefit the wider world is always a big tick in my box marked 'connection'.

Listening to the intuition that was now reverberating louder than my tinnitus, I applied for a place.

A day or so later, an email came back informing me that the trip was sold out.

Damn it. But hey, it clearly wasn't meant to be. And so, I duly forgot all about it.

Until a few weeks later, when another email appeared.

"We've had such an amazing response to the trip, we've decided to run another one. Here are the dates".

The new dates were 10 days after the first one and, coincidentally, the new trip culminated on my 47th birthday.

I took this new information in slowly and decided THIS WAS A SIGN.

I was meant to do this particular trip. To connect to something or someone on this trip.

So, I fired off a quick email to my husband asking could he look after the girls for two weeks while I swanned off to Tanzania to swim with massive fish.

"Pardon?" Came the reply back.

"You want to WHAT??"

"Swim with whale sharks." I replied.

"No, it's not a mid-life crisis. I've already had one of those, got the tattoo and the convertible to prove it too. I need to do this and I want to do this."

Bewildered beyond comprehension, he agreed. I don't honestly think he expected me to go ahead with it. I mean, really, why would I?

And yet, I did mean to go ahead with it.

I Absolutely Wanted To Do This.

This was about something bigger than me. The connection I felt to this trip was tangible.

So here I was, six months later, sat in a hotel restaurant in Dar es Salaam, wondering what the hell I had let myself in for.

The next day, I flew in a tiny (really tiny) plane to Mafia.

Mafia is one of the most beautiful places you will ever see. It's the most culturally original and environmentally natural of Tanzania's Indian Ocean islands, visited by just a few each year.

There is only one road around the island, and the only tarmac on the road is the stretch around the airport. And by airport, I mean the small landing strip and tiny hut that encompasses check in/arrivals, passport control and duty free.

The hotel we stayed in is just outside the capital, Kilindoni. There are no hotels in Kilindoni, in fact, there are only a handful of hotels on the entire island.

Mafia is fortunate to be on the map for two things really: a world-class protected Marine Park and Whale Shark spotting.

Whale Sharks are the gentle giants of the marine world. Fully grown, they can extend as much as 15m in length and little is known about these huge fish as they usually live in the deep ocean. But every year, from October-March, these magnificent creatures can be seen just off the coast of this tiny island and people come from all over the world to see them.

Every morning, we would rise at dawn to head out into the Indian Ocean on the small wooden fishing boat with our guide to look for whale sharks. When our guide spotted them, he would yell "shark" and we would tumble off the side of the rickety boat in our flippers and snorkels to race after them.

And for such huge creatures, they are surprisingly nifty. The first time I came eyeball to eyeball with one was on day two. After being reassured that I was just unlucky not to see one on the first day, I was one of the first on day two to be unceremoniously dumped in the water to make sure I got sight of one.

I will never, ever forget that moment.

Tumbling into the deep water is disorientating enough, with the waves crashing against your skin, but once you right yourself and get your head down, it's a whole different world under the surface.

I put my head down, opened my eyes and looked in front of me. The water was around 15-20 metres deep and crystal clear. I could see the sand on the bottom of the seabed and plenty of other fish swimming nearby. The undersea world was silent. The only thing I could hear was my own breathing against the mask.

And there she was.

About 2 metres down and 20 metres or so ahead, the biggest bloody fish I'd ever clapped eyes on.

And she was heading straight for me.

With no word of a lie, she and I saw each other at the same time. She stared at me, as I stared back at her in awe.

I suddenly remembered to breathe. She swam, slowly and deliberately towards me. Sill looking at me, and I back at her. The gentle waves of the ocean keeping me bobbing up and down in a rhythmic fashion.

We connected. For just a millisecond, we connected. I've never felt a connection like it. And it was magical. This enormous, huge creature with a mouth almost a metre wide could easily have swallowed me whole as a starter. But all she eats is plankton. Lots, and lots, of plankton.

After what felt like an age, but in reality, was probably only a few seconds, I realised that unless I moved pretty damn quickly, I would hit her with my flippers.

We had been warned NOT to be "those tourists". The ones that insist on touching, prodding and poking the wildlife. We were better than that. We weren't tourists. We were conservationists.

So, I took a decision to swim backwards - not easy in flippers, and in hindsight probably not the best move as it didn't really work.

But she was one fin ahead of me. With a small movement of her mighty dorsal, she suddenly turned left, and we lost eye contact as she gracefully passed under me.

I surfaced and raised my hand in the water - elated and excited from my first contact with these almighty creatures as the boat raced towards me to pick me up.

My first experience of whale sharks. And I was humbled and awed by her sheer size, her dominance of the water, but also her gentleness and gracefulness.

During the course of that two weeks, I saw and swam with many other whale sharks, but I will never forget this particular moment and that particular shark.

The connection was real. And when you connect to something outside of you, something bigger than you (literally in this case!), it changes everything inside of you.

That two weeks was one of the most amazing experiences of my entire life. I came home with a renewed sense of purpose and was also humbled by my time in one of the poorest countries I've ever been in. The people of Mafia stole my heart.

Fast forward to now. Here. With me writing this in early April 2021.

I have solid boundaries, in my life and in my business, and I've learned to love myself like my life depends on it. Because it does. Long gone are the dark days where I thought about the end.

It's a cliché used in many a self-development book and trotted out at many a seminar, webinar and coaching programme, but the simple art of giving yourself permission to love yourself deeply is not a destination - one you arrive at and that's it, your journey is over. It's an ongoing journey, that takes twists, turns and some-times U-Turns. It sounds simple, doesn't it? Just love yourself. And it IS simple. But it also requires dedica-tion in difficult times, and it requires commitment when life is going well - so good that you forget you need to keep up your practice.

Since that amazing trip two years ago, I have had the courage and strength to go full-time in my business, during a pandemic. I believe, every single day, that I am enough and we are all connected to something bigger than just what's right in front of us.

In my work as and Transformational Empowerment Coach I have taken myself and my clients on a healing journey to transform, recalibrate and realign; to trans-form themselves from the inside-out in order to maximise their success in life and business.

I have the privilege of creating a business that enables me to work when, where and with whom I choose.

I work with Business Leaders and high-achievers who are already successful - but know deep down that there's MORE.

When you stop disrupting your potential for success by letting your past dictate your future, you create powerful transformations in every area of your life - career, relationships, health, family.

The old adage about fitting your own oxygen mask before helping others is relevant here. And in giving yourself permission to take total responsibility for both your past AND your future, you create space that enables magic to happen.

I'd love to connect with you and hear your story; or empower you to transform, recalibrate and realign your life for the better.

You are meant to have an AMAZING life.

Give yourself permission to empower yourself to live it

ABOUT THE AUTHOR

AMANDA COLES

Amanda is a Transformational Empowerment Coach & NLP Master who helps leaders, entrepreneurs and service-based business owners to transform, recalibrate and realign to magnetically maximise their success in life and business.

Before starting her business, Amanda spent over 20 years as a Leader in People Management. She has also spent nearly a decade as a Transformational Empowerment Coach, Clinical Hypnotherapist & NLP Master. In her work as a Leader in Corporate, she coached everyone informally, from C-Suite Executives to shop-floor workers, and she now brings these unique coaching experiences and perspectives to her business, supporting high-performers who want more from their life and business. Her speciality is empowering people to connect to themselves.

Amanda is also a wife, proud mother to two amazing young women, and owner of a gay dog and an agora-phobic cat. In her spare time, she enjoys reading thrillers and travelling; she particularly loves the Greek Islands.

Amanda can be contacted at:

email: hello@amanda-coles.com

Tel: 0044 (0)7788 230323

Website: https://amanda-coles.com

 facebook.com/amandacoles2

ANNA FAIRS

PERMISSION TO SHAKE YOUR TAIL
FEATHERS

A life less ordinary.

That was always my dream.

And taking a look around me now and reflecting on what I've experienced so far, I think I've accomplished that. And I've a sneaky feeling that the best is yet to come.

I'm an artist, photographer, writer and entrepreneur.

I have freedom, which is my #1 value. I have freedom to be me and follow my passions, wherever they take me. Every day, I can wake up and decide what I want to focus on. If I want to create art, I can. If I want to write, I can. If I want to take an afternoon off because it's a beautiful day and I want to spend some time in nature, I can.

I get to work with the most amazing clients from far-flung places around the globe. I've taken photos for large household names and multiple 7-figure entrepreneurs. My art is hanging in private collections in Denmark, the UK and the US. I help other women take their gifts, passions and talents, and develop irresistible brands; supporting them whilst they launch them into the world.

I've been able to travel with my work and take my son with me too. He's been able to experience different cultures and try out activities he wouldn't have been exposed to if I'd stayed in my previous career. I'm incredibly proud that I've been able to show him that you can create a life you love by following your passions.

Life is precious and short, and our careers take up a huge chunk of that time. What a waste to spend that time doing work you don't love.

I'm so proud that I had the courage to 'climb every mountain.' To find my path, my calling. To chase my dreams and create a life around my passions.

It wasn't always this way though. And I haven't taken the straightest path getting to this point. There've been lots of twists and turns along the way.

How about you? Do you feel like you're on the right path? Or are you feeling stuck and frustrated that life isn't taking you in the direction you want to go? Do you feel that something is missing? That there should be more?

Yes? Then carry on reading. You've stumbled on this book for a reason!

Like my brother and sisters and all my friends, I went to university. But unlike them, I dropped out.

Feeling like a complete failure and not knowing what I could do with my life, I ended up in all sorts of jobs for a while. I worked in a chippy, as a cleaner in an old people's home, as a barmaid, waitress, chef, secretary, directory enquiries operator, international operator, admin assistant at a job centre, office manager for a startup.

Until finally I landed a job in IT.

I took to it like a duck to water and this was my career for the next 18 years. It ticked a lot of boxes for me. I have a curious mind and it was kept busy learning how these complicated systems worked and how to troubleshoot problems when they didn't. I was good at it and it paid well. I moved from operations, where I supported the networks, to design engineering, where I designed networks, to sales, where I sold networks.

The more I studied, the more professional qualifications I got, the more I could earn... which meant I could buy the car, the house, the clothes, the holidays.

I got to travel, meet some cool people and at the time, I was genuinely interested in many of the projects I was working on. I was intentional (as much as I could be) with the type of clients I worked with too, which, for a long time, were public sector organisations as I always wanted to be involved (in however small a capacity) in something that wasn't just about the money. Something worth while. But something was missing.

Although the work was intellectually challenging it didn't **REALLY** light me up.

I poured blood, sweat and tears into it, but I couldn't pour my soul into it. The work left me emotionally and spiritually empty. It was only ever a means to an end. A way to pay the bills. And as I continued to work my way up the pay grades, I found myself more and more unhappy AND wearing a pair of golden handcuffs.

I did get to meet plenty of men though and this is how I met the man I had my son with. It was at this point I started my first business as a portrait photographer, which was life-changing. I suddenly had the creative freedom I'd been craving. Unfortunately, our relationship wasn't a great match and it didn't last. And although my photography business had been growing, I didn't feel secure enough financially to support myself and my son, so I went back to IT.

So now I was a lone parent, in a career that didn't light me up. It wasn't a 9-5 either. It involved long hours and travel and I didn't see Charlie as much as I wanted. I was going through the motions of living. I worked for the weekend and holidays. The money was great. I could afford holidays and buy pretty much whatever I wanted for me and Charlie.

But the price I was paid was unhappiness.

And I numbed this with alcohol. I'd drink wine every evening. Nothing serious, only a couple of glasses. Half a bottle, max. But looking back, I did that nearly every night for fifteen years. Anaesthetising all sorts of emotions and feelings I didn't want to deal with including the frustration I felt for living a life that didn't feel like mine. But what else could I do? I felt trapped into doing the sensible thing. It was a secure, well paid career. I should just suck it up and be grateful for what I had.

The thing is though… life is too short and precious to waste. Do you really want to go through the motions? Do you really want to settle for a career and life that don't light you up?

Which is what I did for so long.

What may come as a surprise to friends and past colleagues is that I spent most of that time feeling like an imposter.

Do you ever have that feeling? That you're going to be found out at any moment? That you've got somewhere through pure luck?

It's a strange, uncomfortable feeling and an interesting topic. I think I experienced it for a few reasons.

Firstly, I was a female engineer in a very male dominated industry. Many of the men I worked with, the majority in fact, were lovely.

So, although I was often the only woman in the room (more so as I worked my way up), I never felt (or suffered from) the discrimination some women have. But I did feel the odd one out. And over the years, I would often ask myself if I was there through merit or if I was the dreaded token woman. It was in the background all the time… had I been hired just to hit some 'politically correct' targets, or was I actually good at my job?

These feelings didn't hold me back though. In fact, like many people with imposter syndrome, they had the complete opposite effect. I allayed the feelings of being an imposter by pursuing a never-ending stream of professional qualifications. To prove to myself, more than anyone else, that I did actually know my stuff, I became certified as a Microsoft Engineer, a Cisco Engineer and a Checkpoint Engineer. With each new position, I'd throw myself into more research and study. Continually learning. Always growing.

I was often surrounded by people that had university degrees and as I'd dropped out, I think this added to the imposter syndrome. At one level, I knew I was just as good as these people, but I think another part of me didn't feel 'good enough'.

Outside of work, I desperately wanted to prove myself to my family and parents too. I come from a family of high achievers: Directors, PhDs, BScs, MScs, a Squadron Leader

The family photos at my parent's house were full of my brother and sisters dressed up in their graduation gowns, and then later, smiling in their wedding photos. But there weren't any of me. I'd failed at both these milestones in life. I'd dropped out of uni and my ex had called off our wedding six weeks before it was due to take place. I was happy for my siblings but yet again, I felt like the odd one out. And although I'd smile and joke about it, deep down I think it affected my self-worth.

Do you ever feel like the odd one out? Amongst your family? Your group of friends? It can be so hard at times but maybe you feel that way for a reason. Maybe you're supposed to be doing something different. Perhaps you haven't found your tribe yet?

As well as feeling an imposter at work, I also sensed I was in the wrong profession. I remember sitting in the various offices, looking around at everyone in their pigpens. To me, the physical environment was dull, sterile and colourless. I remember having urges to sing or shout, or jump somersaults down the corridor. I didn't... but I just remember having this pent-up creative energy inside of me, with nowhere for it to go.

It was pretty confusing for me as I was good at my job and I was getting paid well for it. On so many counts it was a great career with lots of opportunities, and being tech savvy has been a massive bonus for me as I've grown my own business. But ultimately, we weren't a good match and I now realise that I settled for so long in a career and working environment that were toxic to my health and well-being.

I suffered from mental health issues throughout this entire time and was too scared to really open up to anyone about it. It was scary as hell sometimes and I was often holding on for dear life. You wouldn't know from the outside. I kept my nose to the grindstone during the day and drank in the evenings. It was far from the life I'd once dreamt of.

I started a few escape plans. I took evening classes in subjects I was interested in but, as I travelled with work, I'd end up missing so many and found I could never complete a course of study. At one point, I thought my dream job would be interviewing people. I love chatting, learning new subjects and figuring out what makes people tick. I actually joined the team at Manchester Hospital Radio for a while, hoping that could be a stepping stone into a new career. But that's a whole other story!

Looking back, I realise that for so many years, I'd settled for living half a life.

In all areas too. I'd settled for a career that was interesting and well paid, but not really suited to my gifts and passions. It wasn't a good match. I settled for men and relationships that weren't good matches either.

I can see now that I was following the path I thought I had to. College, uni, career, find a partner, settle down. For some reason, I was going through the motions of living out this 'set' path and I was paying a heavy price in terms of my mental and physical well-being.

Sometimes we can only make sense of our lives looking backwards. Hindsight is indeed a wonderful thing! But reflecting on my journey, I think many of my problems, including the imposter syndrome, feeling the odd one out and my mental health issues came from NOT following my creative passions when I was younger.

I was always very creative. Right from an early age, I'd be the one creating elaborate imaginary worlds for my younger sister and I to play in. I painted my parent's furniture green. I cut and 'styled' my hair. I loved reading. And writing. In fact, I have many diaries and poems from my teenage years. I loved art and I spent hours drawing and painting. There was definitely something inside of me that had to come out of me. I'd always had a burning desire to express myself.

At school, my favourite subjects were Art, English Literature and History. I found the sciences interesting and I was good at them. In fact, I was a good all-rounder. But my heart was really with the arts. My father, bless him, was a physicist, and he had a huge passion for his subject. My brother and sister, who were quite a bit older than me, went to uni to study physics. My sister achieved a PhD and my brother came away with a BSc and went on to be a fighter pilot with the RAF.

They were hugely successful figures in my childhood. So, although I don't remember any pressure ever being put on me to pursue the sciences. For some reason, when it came to choosing my A-Levels I chose Maths, Physics and English.

I wish I could remember why. English yes, but the other two? No idea! And that decision impacted the decision I made when it came to going to university.

I think a key thing to add at this point is that my mum is an artist. A very talented artist. She painted miniatures when she was younger and has painted stunning landscapes and scenes with animals. Sadly, my mum won't call herself an artist. She'll only call herself a draftsperson as she feels she only has the talent to copy from a photograph but not paint from her imagination.

We've chatted about this whilst I've been writing this chapter and although I tell her she's an amazing artist, I know she doesn't really believe me. She's never sold any of her work or accepted commissions as she isn't confident enough. Her words.

I don't have time to go into all of it now (perhaps the subject for another book?!) but my mum has suffered with low self-esteem and low self-worth for most of her life. I think a lot of this was passed on to her from her own mother. My grandmother was illegitimate. She never felt loved or wanted as a child and lived quite a sad life.

I used to wonder why all of us children followed in my dad's footsteps but looking back, I can see that although my parents did the best they could, I think they were primarily concerned with helping us make career choices that would lead to 'safe' professions. A career in the arts wasn't anything any of us knew much about. I also think my mum's lack of self-belief in herself, especially in her identity as an artist didn't help the arts as a possible career choice in our house.

So, at 18 I ended up taking the wrong A-levels, which then led to taking the wrong degree. I chose physics. And dropped out. Desperate to do the 'done thing' and get a degree I tried again but only lasted two terms before dropping out again. For a long time, I used to tell myself that I never should have gone to uni. But I truly believe now that if I'd actually chosen something I was passionate about, things would have turned out differently.

As I mentioned earlier, I realised I was on the wrong path many times during my career. But it's so hard once you're on a path to change. Especially the further down that path you go.

I was earning good money. Over $100k towards the end. I was a lone parent. Completely responsible for bringing home the bacon. And I remember the sinking feeling every Sunday evening of having to do the 'sensible' thing and feeling as if my life was passing me by.

I did have conversations with family and friends. Running over ideas of leaving and following a more creative path. And a lot of fear and negativity came up:

"Oh, that's nice to keep as a hobby."

"You'll struggle to make a living from it."

"It's too much of a risk."

"How on earth will you make that work"

"That's something you can pursue when you're retired."

"You'll never give up IT!"

Not really believing them, but not quite ready to jump either, I kept hanging on in quiet desperation.

That was until life threw me a curve-ball. Three in fact. Three moments that changed the course of my life.

The first was when Charlie came along. My son. My gorgeous beautiful boy.

I'd waited for so long to be a mum and he came along and I was so incredibly happy.

I knew I didn't want to go back to work. I wanted to have a job I could fit around raising him. So, I started my first business. Pretty much on a whim. I'd loved photography since school and after taking some photos of Charlie, I decided to set myself up as a photographer. I popped down to the local baby clinic. Handed out some leaflets, put up some posters and booked a room for the following week. I rocked up with all my gear and found I had a queue of mums waiting for portraits. My first clients. I loved growing my business; practicing my craft and learning about sales and marketing. It was with a heavy heart that I had to stop and go back to the corporate world when my relationship with Charlie's father ended.

The second curve ball was when my dad died. I spent most of the last two weeks of his life by his side. He was such a passionate, optimistic man with a huge lust for life. So to watch the life drain out of him as his body visibly wasted away in front of my eyes, and to see him rage against the 'dying of the light' because he wanted to carry on living was heartbreaking.

But going through that very sad and intense experience made me want to live my life. REALLY live it. I didn't want to have regrets. I didn't want to get to the end of my life and not have given it my best shot. I didn't want to settle for going through the motions. I wanted to use my talents, follow my passions and make a difference. So, his death had a huge impact on me and I threw myself into working on my escape plans.

The third moment, though less profound, was the final turning point. It gave me the courage to take that final leap of faith and go all in following my passions. I remember it vividly.

It had been a particularly busy period at work and I'd been working ridiculous hours. 70- 80 hours a week. Anyway, I remember I was sitting in bed, working away on a presentation for a new client at 3am in the morning. And I remember stopping and thinking to myself, "What the fuck am I doing with my life? This isn't a life!"

I spent the rest of the night going round and round in circles wondering if I could pack my career in? Was it the sensible thing to do? Could I make enough to support myself and Charlie? What if I failed?

Morning came and I decided to hand my notice in. It was scary as hell and liberating all at the same time. That was five years ago and my life is a million miles away from what it was like then. I run my own business. And my creativity and artistic spirit are allowed to fly free. I finally have the freedom that once seemed so elusive.

I get to choose who I work with, when I work and what projects I work on. I've also grown a business around raising my son. I've been able to travel for projects abroad and take him with me. I've given him experiences that I once only dreamt about.

I get to plan my days. And if I don't have any pressing commitments, I can decide to take the day off and spend it how I choose. Whether that's walking, reading, listening to music, taking photos or making art. Usually very simple pleasures. But I can go where my mood takes me and to me that's the ultimate freedom.

And this is the level of creative freedom I want for you too.

If you're not happy; if you feel stuck in a career that doesn't light you up; if you know your passions lie elsewhere, I want you to know that you can make a change. In fact, you have my full permission to chase your dreams.

> 'Don't ask what the world needs. Ask what makes you come alive, and go do it. Because what the world needs is people who have come alive.'
>
> — HOWARD THURMAN.

Life isn't something we have to suffer. It's here to be lived and enjoyed. You're allowed to have fun. You're allowed to be creative, to express yourself and share your gifts and talents with the world. You're allowed to be YOU. And you're allowed to shine.

But I do get that it feels hard to do this.

Life can so easily feel like something that happens to us. That we're buffeted around by events beyond our control. That we're victims of our circumstances. And our dreams can seem silly, selfish and something we should simply forget.

But I want you to know that you're more powerful than you think. You can choose a different path.

> "*I am the master of my fate, I am the captain of my soul.*"

— WILLIAM ERNEST HENLEY.

We're not victims. Our souls are unconquerable. And whatever our current circumstances, we can choose to make changes.

I found myself as a single mum, in the wrong career. I could have allowed that to define me. To accept my lot and live half a life. But I didn't. I fought for the life I wanted.

Was it easy? No. Has it been worth it? Absolutely.

My life has opened up in so many ways. Ways I couldn't have even predicted before I started taking steps in the direction I really wanted to go. I've met the most amazing and inspiring women, from all walks of life, not just from the IT bubble I'd been living in. We can become so institutionalised when we're working for one company, within one industry. It's so hard to fully appreciate that there's a whole, wide world out there, just waiting for us to explore.

We can feel small and insignificant at times, but we're actually more powerful than we realise. We get to choose. Every single day. We get to create the life we want. And if we find we're on the wrong path, we're allowed to change our minds. We can make a choice to double back. And take that turning that makes our heart sing.

Every day we get to choose. And it doesn't matter how old you are either. There's always time to choose again.

If you're reading this and feeling like I used to, unhappy, on the wrong path and wanting to start your own business, my signature 1:1 program, SHAKE YOUR TAIL FEATHERS, might be just what you're looking for. I'll help you discover your gifts, passions and strengths. You see, there is only one YOU! You're unique and fabulous! And it's my mission to help you see this in yourself and package up everything you have to offer into a service that your dream clients will find utterly irresistible.

But for now, here are some of the principles I've used to create the life I live. The same ones I take my clients through.

Let's get you back on track and create a business and life around the things that actually light you up.

CURIOSITY

They say curiosity killed the cat but I think curiosity is one of the most important qualities we can have. And I think getting curious is the first step on your path. Get curious about the things you enjoy. What lights you up? What would you do even if you weren't paid? What are your passions? Gifts? Strengths? I think if you follow what brings you joy, you won't be far off the mark. It's like an internal compass. You already know your way. Get curious about how you could make a change. Could you take an evening class? Go part time? Take a sabbatical? Ask yourself empowering questions. How can I make this work? Rather than dismissing ideas that initially seem insurmountable.

CONFIDENCE

We can sabotage ourselves before we've even begun sometimes. Who am I to try this? I'm being silly. What will they think? We all have a mean voice jibber-jabbering away in the background, and it becomes louder and meaner when we start thinking about making changes. It's actually doing its job of trying to keep us safe. So don't listen to that voice. You aren't that voice. Look at all the things you've accomplished in your life so far and stop overthinking it. Take some action. However small. Go confidently in the direction of your dreams. Each step will give you the confidence to take the next one. I sometimes think it's like following a set of clues. One thing leads to the next, then to the next. Have faith and trust yourself *and* the universe to guide you.

CREATIVITY

Having a creative mind is a huge asset when growing a business. In fact, as the wonderful Maya Angelou says, *"You can't use up creativity. The more you use, the more you have."*

So, brainstorm away. You'll come up with creative ways to promote your business, creative sales strategies, creative working practices, creative PR. You'll end up with so many ideas, and then it'll be a matter of picking the good ones and running with them. Or trying one out. Learning from it. Tweaking it. And trying it again. Some will fly, some won't. But it's OK. It's half the fun in fact.

COURAGE

Shortly after handing my notice in, a couple of friends called me brave. To be honest, at the time I wasn't sure if I was brave or stupid, but I do know it took some courage. To take a step into the unknown is a scary thing. But until we take those first steps, we can't see how our adventure will unfold. I always think it's like that scene in Indiana Jones where he can't see the steps across a cavern until he takes the first step. It's normal for us to want certainty. We want to feel safe. But sometimes we just have to be brave and take a chance on life and ourselves. Aren't you worth that? And what's the worst that could happen? You fail. Which is never really a failure as you'll have learnt something. And isn't it better to have tried, and live without regrets, than play it safe and wind up at the end of your life, wishing you'd given it a go? I know which I'd prefer.

Remember you're not doing this on your own. The universe will guide you. The natural state of the universe is one of growth. And it will support your growth too. There's a lovely quote from the Talmud that sums this up beautifully:

> "Every blade of grass has its angel that bends over and whispers, "Grow, grow."

So don't be afraid of change and growth. You're supposed to. You're allowed to.

COLLABORATION

Starting a new business can be pretty overwhelming, especially if we've no prior experience running one. We can muddle along for a while, trying things out and it can be pretty fun. But at some point, we realise that we can achieve more if we collaborate with other creatives, other business owners. This can be finding a community, networking with other business owners, running events/promotions together. It's more fun when you've got a group of friends to grow and celebrate with. And having business friends that understand what you're trying to achieve is so important as you go through the inevitable ups and downs.

I've used all of these principles to start and grow my business and I've gone from selling $20 items through to selling $13k packages.

I started with getting curious on how I could take my skills and passions and create services that would allow me to leave my career. I got curious about my craft. I studied. Practiced. Experimented. And got better. I dreamed up creative ways to promote my business and learnt how to collaborate with local businesses that had the same ideal client. I got out of my own way and took action. I had my doubts and fears, but I didn't let them stop me. I'm a big believer in feeling the fear and doing it anyway. You get confident from taking imperfect action rather than waiting for the day you feel 100% ready.

One of my clients went through a similar process. When we first met, she was working in the corporate world and was pretty unhappy. She didn't feel aligned to the way the company operated and she didn't feel respected or valued. She got curious about her options, the type of business she wanted to create and what clients she wanted to work with. She took massive action despite feeling unsure of herself or the outcome and started a business she loves. She opened her doors in January, has signed five corporate clients and is now working on a book.

Another client has grown her business by embracing her passions and finding the courage to share them with the world. She's been able to show up more consistently, sharing content that's from the heart and in complete alignment with who she is. She's able to call in her dream clients with ease.

Another client applied some of these principles and has gone from selling 1-2 items a month through to selling 2-10 a day. She got curious in terms of really understanding her ideal client and what they actually wanted. This enabled her to create content that deeply connected with their desires. She got curious on how she was currently showing up online and was able to see that a different strategy would work more effectively. She had the confidence and courage to execute on it, without having the proof it was going to work.

So, if you're feeling stuck in a career that makes you miserable, I promise you there is another way. Many creative people find themselves on the wrong path.

Some feel that something is off but can't quite put their fingers on it. Some know deep down that they made some wrong turns a long time ago. Whatever your situation is, life can feel empty and uninspiring when you're on the wrong path.

But there is another way. You can make a living from following your passions. You're allowed to. And I give you permission right now to start believing it's possible for you.

Use the principles I shared earlier. Start with curiosity. Get curious about you and what you'd love to be doing with your life. Then take the first step in that direction, whether that's taking a class, finding out more info, or chatting with someone who is doing what you'd like to do.

Just start. As Henry David Thoreau says;

> *"Go confidently in the direction of your dreams! Live the life you've imagined."*
>
> — HENRY DAVID THOREAU

And if you'd like some support unlocking your unique set of skills, passions and talents, creating a business that lights you up I have 1:1 and group programmes that are designed to do just that. I'll take you by the hand and lead you through the creative process that is branding, and guide and support you as your ideas and business take flight.

You can find more info at www.shakeyourtailfeathers.com or come and join me in my FREE Facebook group www.facebook.com/groups/shakeyourtailfeathers

You see, I've been where you are; wondered if I was being silly. Wondered if it was possible. But I did it. And you can too.

Life is precious. You're precious. Don't waste your time here going through the motions and playing it safe. This is your life. Your time here on earth. Grab it with both hands, chase your dreams and create a life that lights you up.

ABOUT THE AUTHOR

ANNA FAIRS

Anna has been described as a Renaissance woman and working with her, it's easy to see why. Her insatiable curiosity, combined with experience in different disciplines, has fuelled her creative mind and her infectious energy spills over into everything she touches. She'll infuse some magic into your branding but keep everything grounded by pairing it with practical, powerful and proven strategies.

Anna worked for 18 years in the corporate world, from engineering positions to sales and business consultancy, working with well-known household names including

Lockheed Martin, UN World Food Programme and the British Council.

Anna enjoys the great outdoors, travelling and reading.

Anna is available for branding projects, art collaborations and commissions.

You can reach Anna at:

Email - anna@shakeyourtailfeathers.com

Website - www.shakeyourtailfeathers.com

You can view Anna's artwork at www.annafairs.com

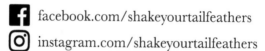 facebook.com/shakeyourtailfeathers
instagram.com/shakeyourtailfeathers

PERMISSION TO PLAY TO YOUR STRENGTHS

I'm me. Amazing me with ADHD as I have started to call myself! I've achieved a lot in my life up to now and do you know what? I don't think I'll ever slow down. Instead, I see myself as someone who celebrates life. I'm hungry for opportunities and often seek out new challenges because I love to test myself, learn, and explore. I don't like missing out.

I'm incredibly proud to have started my own global, award-winning skincare brand. My frustration and inquisitiveness about the lack of available products fuelled my passion to want to change things, to want to change the world. So, I worked hard to make it happen. I embrace the tough stuff; it spurs me on. I believe I have grit and tenacity which compliments my curiosity. This has helped me no end, and steers me forward.

My entrepreneurial journey didn't start with skincare though. I've been in business for almost 20 years. I've owned multiple types of businesses. From property to beauty and skincare, including an international company spanning the Middle East, USA, Australia, and Europe. It actually started off as a small one-room beauty salon I bought from eBay. I also owned the oldest estate agency in Liverpool. I've created businesses from scratch, with no funding, and taken over a 150-year-old business that was on its knees and turned it into a thriving business within 3 years.

Getting through a day can be a monumental battle and I can't always plan or schedule. But I've accepted this is what my life is like and I'm content. Every day is different and I don't know what type of day I'm going to have to face. I wouldn't change it because it's bursting with excitement, opportunity, love, and unpredictability.

It has always been drummed into me that I had to make something of myself. I can vividly recollect this, even from a tender age. That was kind of the measurement of a successful life for my family. I can honestly feel like I have done well, but it certainly wasn't by doing it the conventional way. There was no straight road ahead for me, even though it feels like that's often instilled in us - there's just one straight road ahead and you must follow it. Mine was a very winding road; a rollercoaster with lots of differing heights, up and down, obstacles coming out of my ears - that's the kind of road life has served me. Many times, I've crashed into barriers, but have managed to find a way around them.

All of my life, I have been in jobs and surrounded by run-of-the-mill people. You must know the type I am referring to; they're all on a conveyor belt of a step-by-step, mapped out plan of how to get ahead in life. Think Stepford Wives, or clones. The mantra they would bleat out after having had it programmed into them was always the same:

- Get as many qualifications as you can in school,
- Leave school,
- Get a job, any job, bring in your own money and stand on your own two feet – hopefully it's a good company and you will get a pension,
- Meet a boy,
- Get into a relationship at a very young age,
- Get engaged,
- Plan the wedding of the century that you're still paying off 20 years later,
- Buy a house,
- Within two years, first baby,
- Within five years, second baby,

- Let's hope you have one of each sex, like everyone else, as life is just perfect then. As someone said, this is what a perfect life is all about.

Well, excuse me, but who wrote this book of rules? Who said this is what you should learn at school? Who said this is what you have to do? I was well aware early on that conformity was never going to be a strong point. It was never going to be a given as I trotted through life. No Stepford Wife role for me I'm afraid. It's mind-boggling to think that you had to be like everybody else to fit in and be successful. That you should keep your head on and play the role already set out for you and it'd all work out fine in the end!

I encourage you to break the mould. Smash it, bend it, throw it against the wall, rip it up, just make sure you make your own. One just for you and your wonderfully superb life. Dare to be different and see how exciting and fulfilling everything becomes. That's all that matters. That's what I would have said to little Ashley. I'd say, "Be you and you alone. Do it your way and you will be just fine."

I didn't always have the confidence to be myself and I always felt like I had to prove myself to others. For me, it was definitely a case of attempting to convince myself I was just as good as other people. I just could not shake this off and it made a defined indentation on my brain. Trouble is, I never truly felt I was as good as all the rest and this stuck with me for such a long time. I wanted to be like them. They appeared to have it all sussed out, so why wasn't I like them? What was wrong with me? How come I couldn't match even my own weighty expectations? A barrage of questioning infiltrated my thoughts; was it my looks? The shape of my body? Being tall when everyone else was small (in proportion for their age)? I was sticking out like a sore thumb for all the wrong reasons. A deep-rooted belief that something was amiss was obvious, yet went ignored and unnoticed.

How I managed to function like this is beyond the realms of my own understanding, yet it seemed to be the done thing to believe such so-called truths. When you are only shown one way, then that way is how you live and move forward. It's accepted as a given and you daren't ever question because then you would stick out, and why would you want to do that? This is very much the way of thinking that was subconsciously conditioned into my brain from day dot. I find that this kind of programming can be both detrimental and lethal. Do we ever really fully let go of our hardened belief system? Will there be long-lasting residue we can never get rid of?

This very glaringly apparent lack of self-belief was just embedded in me. It was something that ran through my veins from a very early age and it just seemed to be a conveyor belt. Imagine the conflict inside me when I realised that I knew I was different. It was tough to juggle such inner thoughts. I wasn't like everybody else and I had a loud voice in my head basically saying as much. It was highly critical and, for the life of me, I couldn't lower the volume, let alone mute it. That is a lot for anyone to have to cope with, let alone a small child, confused and unsure about how they slotted into the world. Your head drops and you can never quite bring yourself to lift it and hold it unashamedly high.

My lack of self-worth came through in everything I did and with every part of my life for many, many years. I was a failure at everything I did or wanted to do. I think this is due again to how we are taught and led to believe what life should be all about. Sadly, there were no cheerleaders fighting my corner and driving me on, doused with hearty encouragement and "Bravo Ashley". There was no other alternative door to knock on, or route to wander along. That was it. Failure equated to failure, pure and simple.

So, I knew I was unique, but I couldn't quite articulate how and why. It's tough to understand what you believe and fear what can't be understood. I mean, where does that lead? All I craved was to be good and successful at what I wanted to do, to make people proud, and to fit in and be part of the crowd. My opinion of myself wasn't up to scratch. How could it have been when I knew I wasn't like the rest of the herd. I felt like one of the Raggy Dolls, and would be tossed aside as categorically defected to the point of no return. Such monumental pressure to be under the spell of! This has always haunted me, because I was still learning my way, as are all children at that age. Children are hugely influenced by all the external environments they come into contact with, and everything they are told they will listen to, even if it doesn't seem like it. What I saw around me shaped my psyche.

As I was growing up, the usual question that everyone would ask would be, "What do you want to be when you grow up?", "A nurse", I would say. Obviously, wanting to care for people was evident from such a young age. A garage sale was taking place and there was a nurse's outfit being sold. Make no mistake, I wanted the outfit like I've never wanted anything before. I couldn't wait to attend the sale. The original plan was that if you worked there then you could pick one item that was for sale and I knew I had to get there early for the nurse's uniform to claim it as my reward for working. I knew my mum wouldn't give me the money but I had a solution on how I was going to get it. But then, all of my dreams were shattered.

Two brain boxes from school, both called "Gillian", said I could help out behind the counter but then they gave me a maths test to see how I could add up and take away, which I failed miserably. They then said I couldn't help! My heart was in a million pieces and I was so ashamed of myself that I couldn't even bring myself to go and see what was going on at the garage sale when it took place. I watched from round the corner behind a wall and watched everything that went on. I didn't want to go as I was scared that people would ask why I wasn't behind the counter. I also think that they had been laughing at me and telling everyone about how badly I did in the maths test they gave me. It was one of the most horrible experiences of my life; I still think about it today and the long-lasting effect it had on my self-esteem and confidence.

Now, I have to talk about an old teacher called Mrs. Donnelly. I can most definitely say that she hated me because she plainly did and didn't really attempt to hide it! I know that she would bad mouth me so much to my mum, Dolly, that I lied about there not being any parent's evening, so she wouldn't hear the things that she would say about me. It was necessary for me to do this as I literally was living in fear of her spewing venomous and unfounded accusations against me. Maybe she wanted to rile me, well she absolutely succeeded on that front. My desk was untidy and Dolly was horrified. Mrs. Donnelly was determined to see

Dolly though. She kept on asking me and I kept on saying that Dolly didn't want to attend. I was petrified of her, just because I could feel she didn't like me. Her dislike towards me oozed out of every pore she had. I could see it in her face. That scenario has always made me feel uncomfortable and, to be honest, shaken. This was a teacher whose job it was to nurture and educate me, not to belittle and chastise me for no reason other than, what I can only surmise, was her own entertainment. Looking back, I have thought about that innocent little girl who had dreams, and wish that I could wrap my arms around her and tell her that it doesn't matter. Every single person is different and unique.

When I think about what events and life experiences made me believe in these false truths then, if I'm honest, I think about all the times when I tried about, what felt like, a million jobs. I would flit from one company to another and ended up in a cycle doing this. There always happened to be a voice in my head that would start to repeat the same information. It was like it was speaking to me, saying that there's something more for you, that this isn't you, that you don't like doing this, that you don't fit in, that this is where you don't want to be. That voice became one of the ever presents in my life, and formed part of my habitual routine. I couldn't dial it down, I accepted it. I wondered if anyone else had it. Was it a normal occurrence? It got to the point where it used to speak to me very loudly whenever I had got a new job. This was quite the norm at this stage, as I often got myself into a situation where I couldn't physically take doing the old job. So, I'd move on, in the vain hope it would actually make a difference and a false belief that maybe the next job would be better suited to who I was. I call my inner voice Beryl the Feral. Like clockwork, on the first day of every new job, Beryl would pipe up and say, "What are you doing here? What is going on?" And I would long to be back in that old familiar place that I knew.

Something inside was always eating away at me. I envied people who knew what they wanted to be; who said from a young age, I want to be a teacher, and that's what they did and went on to become a teacher for 55 years until the age of retirement. I struggled with not being able to make that decision. I think that if I'd have seen it for what it actually was, I would have been much more happier and content with my choices in life and said to myself, it's not forever, it's to gather knowledge and experience so that you can fill your tool bag for the bigger things that are coming your way. But instead, I was on this search for something to satisfy me and make me like all the rest. I wouldn't have panicked had I known that there was a point to it all.

Was there a lightbulb moment or a wake-up call? A moment I decided or realised that enough was enough? That life wasn't meant to play out this way? That I simply couldn't drag myself along with a crushed spirit, no purpose, aimlessly trying to fit it? I suppose it was a wake-up call really. When I was having my daughter Beth, I got preeclampsia and was very ill. In fact, I could have come close to losing my life. Although it was me who was sick and not Beth, they were far more concerned with her needs primarily and would quite happily have sent me packing despite me suffering and in pain. Throughout my life, I'd become resilient and was the type of person who would do anything they'd set their mind to.

Shortly after this experience, maybe three months or so, I was soaking in a hot bath. I had an opportunity to reflect and contemplate. I knew that my life was on hold and what I was going through. I wanted so much to be healthy, it was making me feel that I wanted to, finally, expose the falsehoods once and for all. It had blighted me immensely up until that point and I guess you can say that I had reached breaking point. I believed that it was now or never, now or die if you like. It was that pivotal moment to turn those tables, to take back control and empower myself to do what was in my heart and soul. I knew I had to change; the thought of carrying on haunted me and it didn't sit right with me. That time had come. Time to be Ashley, to be me and be free.

Conjuring up strength and power I didn't think was possible, I made the heartfelt decision to break up with my partner, Keith. It felt like a cloud had miraculously lifted. All the anger was gone and I was finally breaking the chains. You know what, it felt good and was very cleansing. I was determined to get out and do something for me, to make a life for myself and not be held back by whatever had gone on in the past. I also think I had another lightbulb moment. When Beth reached her teens, she became really sick and it was apparent that she had mental health issues which had gone unnoticed when she was younger. Beth was diagnosed with ADHD. We were advised that it was genetic so I was also tested, and that's when I was diagnosed with ADHD. Talk about a jaw-dropping and life-affirming moment.

That's when it all started to make sense. An awful lot of things started to fall into place. I now realize, looking back, that's why I wasn't like all the rest. I was built differently, my mindset was different, so I didn't accept and be content with any of the so-called golden rules or techniques. Once this truth bomb was well and truly dropped, I became more self-accepting. I was different, but so what? I now knew why that was. I believed in myself, developed confidence and my self-esteem rose like a phoenix from the ashes. I started to listen to what my body was telling me. It made an instant and dramatic change to all aspects of my life. I treated myself with the courtesy and patience I deserved. I did things my way and that way worked. It was like being unleashed with a fresh outlook, a freeing one which allowed me to be the person I had yearned to be, to be Ashley who had been imprisoned inside and shackled for so long.

My success gathered pace and I was able to make my mark in business and in life. I wasn't going to be messed with anymore, lied to, or held back. I can't tell you how liberating it was. I had literally gone from suffering constant knock-backs and put-downs, to making waves as an entrepreneur, being highly respected, and inspiring others which, to me, is a dream.

I repeatedly ask myself, who wrote these rules? Who said that we have to learn XYZ - which probably is never going to be of any benefit to anyone? My advice to anyone would be to rip up the rule book. I mean, come on, who decided they were set in stone anyway? Is it not better to encourage others to find their own way in life? If you asked two people to find their way to the end of a pitch-black road, where one of them used a torch and one didn't have one but felt their way to the end by crawling on their hands and knees, who is to say that the one who crawled did it wrong? They both got there by using their own methods and by trusting themselves to do it the right way. Who is to determine and judge if something is done correctly or incorrectly? You literally have to feel your way in this life. We will make poor judgements, decisions and mistakes, but they are ours and ours alone to make. Let's stop passing opinions on those who do things differently. In fact, let's go out of our way to do it another way, to prove it works and you should never lose faith and hope. What can be done, will be done. Let's just leave it at that.

We are not taught, in the most vulnerable and absorbing time of our life, that we should learn to love ourselves, to acknowledge our feelings and listen to what your body is telling you. One thing which is certain is that we can never run away from ourselves. We have to face who we are head-on, to confront our innermost thoughts, our demons, what makes us tick, what makes us scared. The only person we have to face in the mirror is ourselves. I encourage my clients to look at themselves in the mirror and to not shy away from it. To stare down insecurities, flaws, and weaknesses. They are part of what makes us unique. I tell them to celebrate the flaws like they're going out of fashion. I tell them it's okay to feel like rubbish and to have days when they retreat under their duvet. We all need that time to reboot and replenish our soul. It's allowed, and will help boost us in the long run.

Skincare and aesthetics have played such a major part of my life for the last 10 years, the skincare is prob one of the hardest things I have ever done. I have worked with thousands of clients all over the world and I explain to them that your skin is like a snowflake, like your fingerprint, no-one else has the skin you have, it's unique to you. It's amazing in what it does, it's wafer thin and it holds every part of you together. Your skin is like bricks and mortar. It's built with tiny pieces of skin flakes and they are so delicate and small for the human eye to see, they are held together with a protein, and it's this protein that is the mortar, that keeps it all together".

It's fascinating. Its job is monumental but so many of us don't give it a seconds thought. Your skin is an extension of your immune system, it indicates when something is wrong with you internally or externally, it's unreal. So, treat yourself like a snow flake. You're different, so very important and vital. You have a huge part to play, even if you don't realise it. Once you acknowledge this, I guarantee you will feel lighter and brighter. Don't let the judgement of others hold you back. Imagine what you could be capable of. Mind-blowing.

I want to hear teachers and parents shouting to the children, "you don't have to feel like a square peg in a round hole! All you have to do is learn about you.

Listen to what your body is saying and allow yourself to be strong and not pushed into something, or being someone, you don't want to be. Be strong. Don't put up with struggling through life, we only get ONE and it goes awfully fast, believe me, so make it matter and be happy." Never do you hear the teacher shout, "Go on, learn how to play to your strengths." I think about the boy who wants to play with the bricks and blocks and wear the Bob the Builder hard hat and high vis coat all day long, who is now being sent to the headmaster for being in trouble for not nailing himself to the chair and learning about letters which he can't understand or comprehend, who now has to face his mum for not being able to be at the same level as everyone else in the class and feels, at the tender young age of 5-6, that already he is a massive disappointment and failure for his brain being different.

Mental health is now becoming an epidemic but yet we don't know HOW to deal with it other than medication, which incidentally, when being prescribed you are warned it can cause suicidal thoughts as just one of the side effects. Shouldn't we look at the root of the problem and try to address things a lot earlier? I'm a huge advocator in acknowledging when we might be experiencing poor mental health, but also understanding why. Yes, I know that there are some conditions in which you will think, feel or behave in a particular way with no trigger or reason, but if this is known then it will at least give some reassurance. Suppressing and numbing with meds might provide light relief, but it's about tackling any issues and addressing them, so people can perform and function effectively and be the best version of themselves.

When I see that younger me, that little girl sitting in hell with her whole life in front of her, it makes me sad and makes me cry. All I want to do is wrap my arms around her and tell her that it will be alright in the end and you don't have to be like all the others. This is what I would love to do to those suffering, lacking confidence and purpose. I'd love to show them it's going to be alright.

I would like to point out that I have done the most impulsive things over the course of my life. I bought a business, then didn't want it. I've developed businesses internationally and didn't know what to do then. I worked so hard to get visas for Australia and moved us all there, then once we got there and found somewhere to live, I wanted to come home. I was always chasing a dream, a wish, but never knowing what it was exactly I was chasing or wanting to find. I think I was always looking for an answer and looking for a part of me that so many other people seemed to find and be on the straight and narrow path through life. How come they are so satisfied with life, I often wondered, while attempting to do it their way. However, obsess over that for too long and you'll sorely miss out on opportunities and chances.

I now know that only I can make myself happy by doing what I think is right, what makes my eyes smile and my heart sing. It's empowering when you realise that it's alright to dip in and out, to dive head-long into a new venture or scheme, then decide it's not for you. It's how we learn. I'm proud I have dabbled in so much because I've acquired so much experience and lessons you wouldn't be able to pay for in any business school in the land. I'm all for getting stuck in and getting my hands dirty. I'm an inquisitive creature, always wanting to know how it's done, and the best way is to just get on with it.

I know what's right for me at that moment, but things and circumstances easily change. Something that's right now may not be right further down the line. I've discovered that it's okay. It's easy to mock those who get involved and then lose interest or move into another one. It's perfectly fine to do that. I used to think I was flakey and unreliable, but I'm not. Life might be unpredictable but, to me, it's fulfilling to lead an exciting life. Isn't it what it's all about?

I have ADHD and I've adapted around it because it certainly lets you know when it doesn't want to go along with what you're planning. I'm learning all the time how to deal with it, and it'll take me the rest of my years. However, rather than shun it, I've invited it in from the cold and allowed it to enhance and compliment who I am, and never deter me from doing what I want or achieving success. It's my best friend rather than my worst enemy or nosey neighbour who won't move from staring at me through the window. It's given me licence to still reach my aspirations and goals, even if my journey is fiddly. I'm always finding my way, but I'm loving it.

What I believe I can bring to this party is hope. That there are ways to accomplish and achieve way beyond the realms of what you think you are capable of. You may well think there is no chance, but I have proven that opportunities are abundant, even if you have a complex condition like ADHD. We are known to many as the write-offs. The naughty kids who sit at the back whose lives won't add up to much. They think we get so hyper and muddled, we just walk round in circles and never actually do anything of substance. I'm here to proudly announce that this is not true. We are here to stay, we are here to not just make ripples, but to orchestrate our own tsunami of success.

Stick with what I've written, I can assure you I will have had a good go at convincing you that you can do anything despite adversity, despite a barrage of setbacks and challenges. That with a wonky brain that doesn't always behave or function the way you want it to, you can still make it happen. You'll acknowledge that even with difficulties, you can still do what you want to do. It won't be easy but where's the fun in that? If you embrace uncertainty and feel compelled to take a risk or two, you'll do just fine. You don't have to force yourself to fit in and to be a square peg in a round hole. Instead, we can be loud and proud about breaking the chains of being imprisoned in a life that's not suited to us. We get to decide what's right and how we run things. Be at peace with the real you, be upfront and accepting, and you will flourish in life and business.

ABOUT THE AUTHOR

ASHLEY CAHILL

Ashley Cahill is an entrepreneur, author and business mentor who supports and teaches people with ADHD. She is the proud creator of "Amazing Me with ADHD" and is a powerful leader for women in business with ADHD. She is busy creating a movement that enables people to feel empowered and to realise that having ADHD is a superpower, which lets them develop their own skills and knowledge to turn their passion into a profitable thriving business.

Before Ashley herself was diagnosed on 1st July 2020, she was the owner of multiple businesses in various industries, from property and aesthetics to developing her own skincare range. Ashley describes herself as a "risk taker". She once purchased the oldest estate agents in Liverpool which had been trading then for 150 years, despite having no experience in the housing industry at all, then bought a small nail bar off Ebay on her credit card for a very small amount of money and transformed it into an international company spanning the UK, USA, Middle East and Australia. She has now developed her own skincare range which consists of a 24kt Gold Oil range which is very popular in the Middle East. Ashley then described herself as being someone who sells gold and oil to the Arabs.

Prior to this chapter, she would describe herself as a "Job jumper", never sticking to one job for very long or some even showing up on the second day, and who would have thought that it was all down to having ADHD. Ashley is now proud to be working on projects with the ADHD Foundation to support school leavers wanting to develop their skills and knowledge.

Ashley also enjoys breeding therapeutic perfect puppies to support families with daily challenges from ADHD, but also loves to spend time creating new things that she thinks will improve the lives of others and make things easier.

You can reach Ashley at

ashley@amazingmewithadhd.com

Website www.amazingmewithadhd.com

 facebook.com/ashleycahill

instagram.com/ashley_cahill__

BEVERLEY FRAY

PERMISSION TO BREAK THE CYCLE OF SETTLING, DO YOURSELF JUSTICE

J experienced an awakening moment which was to change my life forever. It was the realisation that, for so long, I had been living in the same cycles and going around in the same circles of life. I wanted to experience more and something had to change to be able to make that happen.

From that day forward, I made the choice to break the cycle without compromise. It was as if I had received my very own personal message from the universe; 'Beverley, this is your time to become FEAR-LESS and you're ready for the next step'.

I made it my personal mission to begin supporting women in overcoming the repeating cycles which have been holding them back for far too long. I began to bridge the gap in helping them to create the necessary change through empowering conversations; establishing what it was that was really holding someone back, discovering who my clients truly are, what they strive for and providing a supportive safe space for breakthroughs and realisations to evolve. Together we become the cycle-breakers.

So, as we dive a little deeper into my story and how I got here, you'll soon know why I'm now firmly on the pathway to saying YES to life again - stepping fully into doing things my way, for three reasons, three core values and one BIG promise which is at the heart of my desires to create more quality time for all the things I care most about:

Time. Time is one of the most precious commodities and is something that we can never get back; nor is it something that should ever be taken for granted, I am grateful for that.

Wisdom. To guide and support others on their journey through life, business, or their career.

Legacy. To leave a legacy that will not only impact my family, but will also create a catalyst for change in the hearts and minds of those whose lives I touch with my vision and mission to create a ripple effect of cycle breakers.

The promise. To be the voice who is empowering one million women to speak up, speak out and break free, to become the powerhouse they were destined to be.

We all know that we make and create our own success. For me personally, it has come in so many different forms; recognition for services to charities, church work, awards for leadership and inspiration in coaching and mentoring. I'm humbled and honoured to have also won awards as part of Inside Out 4 Beauty, which supported communities in creating healthier lifestyles and incorporating a more holistic approach to living.

My biggest success and achievement I've ever accomplished is that I was able to start a family at 40, and it's without doubt why I firmly believe in miracles.

At this early point you may already be thinking that this all sounds very easy, straightforward and 'run of the mill', but let me reassure you that there are so many experiences which have meant that my journey to transformation hasn't always been sunshine, butterflies and rainbows. In fact, there have been more times than I can count when life wasn't clear cut or smooth sailing, but these circumstances don't have to be what forms our future decisions, feelings and choices.

REAL life is a roller coaster of events, situations and setbacks which dictate our reality at the time. Our hope for better outcomes, more luck and transformation is often swept along with "I'll be happy when..." or "I'll start when..." - but more often than not, 'WHEN', never arrives. Of course, we set our goals, intentions and willingly hold onto the belief that everything we want will manifest itself into reality. Sometimes it happens and yet at other times, it seems like an impossibility.

I share this because I feel extremely fortunate to have had a successful career within the world of banking and finance. I was also able to purchase my first home in 1987 and felt on top of the world. But with that high, soon after came an all-time low; I was made redundant.

It left me wondering why on earth this was not working? How come I had followed all the rules - got an education, started out in a career, worked hard, bought a property - and yet I was in a constant state of uncertainty? The interest rates at the time had also doubled and I was unemployed. It was one of the scariest times of my life and this is when I started to lose every ounce of confidence and self-belief as I couldn't see a way forward. Everything seemed so unclear.

Searching for work left me feeling depleted and exhausted as the daily rejection took its toll. It was hard to deal with and I couldn't see a way out. I decided that 'WHEN' had to be 'NOW' and made a conscious choice right there and then that rather than sitting at home on my rusty dusty, feeling sorry for myself and making excuses, I decided to redesign my life and totally change direction.

I volunteered for a charity and at the same time, I trained in The Art of Massage Therapy. This taught me that as well as looking after other people, self-care was just as important too. I felt inspired and motivated to start taking care of myself a little more, which gave me a fresh perspective on what life could look like outside of the banking world.

This all happened at the time when I noticed just how many people were starting businesses and many of them, like myself, had left school with little or no qualifications and yet they were having great success. I intuitively thought 'what if I don't follow the rules and instead play the game of life on my terms?'. It was a feeling I couldn't shift, yet I ignored it.

Shortly after this I was offered interviews by Reuters and other organisations in the City of London; yet after that overwhelming feeling of wanting to start living life more on my terms, I made the decision that I would never take on full-time employment ever again and, for any part-time hours that I worked, I would adopt the mindset of an 'Intrapreneur', a name I gave to my new found commitment to improving any workplace in which I was to be part of. It was my opportunity to cultivate momentum in building positive relationships with my employer and colleagues, and treat my job as if it were my own business which offered a VIP standard to those who used our services.

My invention and intervention of the 'Intrapreneur' allowed me to go on to implement this methodology whilst working for three different charities over a period of 29 years. It's something I am incredibly proud of creating, as it's now been adopted by my peers, colleagues and clients within the corporate space.

Even now, within all the work I still do today, when working with my corporate clients and employees, I introduce them to these 'Intrapreneur' techniques to help them be aware of and have accountability for their actions, but also to commit to enhancing their workplace experiences and relationships in the same way I did, using these proven techniques.

Although I've taken so much joy from empowering others in the workplace and I've enjoyed all the roles and responsibilities I've taken on so far, I've also encountered some challenges which were hard to face the reality of.

Computers. It sounds so simple but computers created a very real issue for me.

Whilst I thrived within a team and I'm a people person, a great communicator and was (and still am) highly regarded by all the clients and customers that I come into contact with, as soon as I was asked to sit in front of a computer and enter information onto that flickering screen, everything instantly became a blur.

This very quickly became a significant problem. Whilst these computerised systems, processes and procedures were speeding up with this new-found technology, I was somehow slowing down and unable to keep up the number of case files which needed to be entered onto this machine which sent me into complete word blindness.

My offline work and customer facing work continued to thrive but, with any type of computer work I did, mistakes started to happen, and my productivity became slower. It was highly stressful and problematic because I couldn't understand why this was happening. I just couldn't keep up and felt I couldn't do this type of role anymore.

This went on for a few months until I was faced with disciplinary action which shocked me to the core. I was devastated to be nearly 50 and, having always been the person called upon to take on all these different projects and tasks, I was being given a warning because I couldn't keep up with the work.

A significant moment came when I was asked to meet with the Company Director to discuss the chain of events and the concerns they had. When I tried to give my explanation and ask for help, the words I heard shuddered through me:

66 'You just need to be resilient.'

These words were thrown back at me and in that moment, as I stared down the lens of the laptop, I was speechless. I didn't break the silence either as there was absolutely nothing more to be said. In that very moment, I saw everything clearly.

Enough was enough and it was time for me to regain my inner strength, take back my power and step forward. I found my voice to speak up and reminded myself of the journey of self-discovery I had been on so far. This experience had just broken the cycle of some of the biggest limiting beliefs I'd faced in my life. I had discovered my resilience and so much more.

I stood in my power and asked to be professionally assessed as something was wrong and I needed support. At this point, I wasn't afraid to ask for the help needed to ensure that I can produce at my best work. I have never limited myself and I was not about to let someone else limit me now. Thankfully, they had a duty of care to take my concerns seriously and referred me for tests which would establish what help was required in order for me to do my job effectively, which is all I ever wanted to do for myself and others.

Following this horrendous meeting, I walked into the bathroom, stood directly in front of the mirror, I looked at myself squarely in the eyes and I just let the tears flow.

Why was I crying uncontrollably?

It was the knowledge that I was asking for help which, without a fight, would have been denied. There are times when we have to allow our raw emotions to come up to the surface so that we don't suffer in silence and now I know for sure that my emotions are the fuel for my fire.

That day, I released my fears. I realised my emotions and stared life in the face. There was no chance that I was going to allow this incident to create bitterness on any level; I had to confront it head on. I wanted to deal with the reality of what had just unfolded and find the blessing in what had been said. And it was a blessing.

It had taken me years to get to that point. To make the decision to stop hiding in the shadows and to use my voice, not just for myself but in advocacy for clients. Still standing, looking in the mirror, I asked myself:

Is my work finished here?

If I stay, what will the consequences be?

I carried on, probably because it felt like the path of least resistance at the time. A week after my 50th birthday I was diagnosed with dyslexia - an outcome I was relieved to find, as at least now this answered so many of the questions, put my mind at ease and confirmed that I needed support in the workplace.

It was actually during this time that I was able to break free from one of my biggest limiting beliefs. It was from seeking help, learning and discovering more about myself at a deeper level that allowed me to stand in my power.

From one of the lowest and most difficult times of my life, I discovered more about myself than I had ever imagined, I discovered that RESILIENCE was in fact strongly rooted within my DNA. I had always felt this but now I actually really knew and understood that this was the game changer for me. It felt like this had to happen to enable me to support others through difficult times like this so that they never felt as alone as I did. It was part of the transformation required for my next chapter of life.

The challenges I had faced had contributed to a collection of blocks and limiting beliefs that had held me back for what felt like my whole life. Finally, I was able to break free from them.

The issue I had was that I still had to do the same job and the same work, so would still be in the same cycle of stress and anxiety from trying to keep up. I didn't want to do that anymore and, on making the decision to hand in my resignation, on that very same day I was head-hunted for project work which was perfectly aligned with the direction I wanted to go.

Suddenly, so many opportunities started to present themselves. It was like I had cut the cord of limitation and I could explore the types of roles which were more purposeful and valuable to those who needed my expertise. One of the most rewarding projects I went on to thrive with was creating a program for aiding and equipping over 150 individuals with mental health issues, drug and alcohol addiction who were in hostels; to help them regain their self-worth and independence to integrate back into a healthier living environment and to become self-sufficient within their own life.

This was such a rewarding, beautiful process as it became a journey of rediscovery for me too. This included going back to my roots of finance and money breakthrough and tapping back into that soul calling of wanting to 'dip my toe' into the world of entrepreneurship. So, I decided to combine three decades worth of wisdom, knowledge, training, work and life experience to further educate myself and become an ICF Accredited

Coach, professionally qualified in wellness, career, team and executive coaching; specifically focusing on Life Transformation and Money Breakthrough Coaching.

After all this self-discovery and education, you might think this is where the big breakthrough moment comes in, but actually, for the next few years, I settled back into life. Having overcome the difficult situations life had thrown at me, having done all 'the work', I just went back to continuing on and going back into the same repeating cycle of holding myself back from what I was truly capable of.

It wasn't until I saw the movie "I Know Why The Caged Bird Sings", by Maya Angelou, that things changed. In the film, she tells her own childhood story. Within it is a scene that moved me beyond words and it still brings a quiver in my voice today. A little girl is depicted, stuffing socks into her mouth to stop herself from feeling the pain, anguish and hurt of her child-hood trauma. A trauma which resonates deeply with every inch of my soul.

That little girl stopped herself from talking for years, because she realised that WORDS HAVE POWER and when she had spoken up, it had been costly. This had not only reminded me of my own childhood trauma, but it also allowed me to reflect upon the words spoken in that meeting where I was told to 'have more resilience'. Just by watching this extremely poignant film, something within me switched ON.

I was never going to be made to feel small again.

I wasn't going to keep quiet, just to please others.

I do have a birth right to tell the truth about how I feel.

It was my time to make a change, once and for all.

I suddenly remembered how precious life is and found memories of the past resurfacing like a reminder and reason for me to start living into the vision which I had created 10 years ago. As I found myself looking back on my life, it was like watching a replay of these life moments which could have been so different. It could have been so tragic.

The life-movie which was playing out in front of me so clearly was Saturday, 17th December 1983. I was 21 and was always so self-assured, growing in confidence, full of energy and had a positive outlook on life. I was studying a BTEC National in Business and Marketing and worked part time at 'The Worlds Leading Luxury Department Store', the one and only Harrods in Knightsbridge, London.

That Saturday an IRA bomb exploded in a car outside the department store. Six people died and 97 were seriously injured that day, and so many more could have been injured and killed, including me. Escaping from the building with colleagues and customers as the windows blew in and smoke filled each of the departments, to survive was nothing more than a miracle. Another reason why I believe in miracles.

Still in shock, the next morning as I travelled to Heathrow airport to board a flight to New York, I promised myself that I was not going to play it small in life, my studies or path to my future career. It was a miracle I survived, and life is too precious to waste a moment of it.

BAM! Ouch! It hit me like a slap in the face because here I was, all these years later, having the same thoughts and making the same promises yet doing nothing about it and staying in the same repeating cycle. This wasn't the only example, so I knew in that moment that THIS was the message I needed to hear. It was the universe SCREAMING AT ME to make the change.

As I stood there, annoyed with myself, debating what to do and wondering how so many years had passed with me repeating these same cycles, I remembered one of the most powerful books I have ever read, 'Better Decisions, Fewer Regrets - 5 Questions to help you determine your next move, by Andy Stanley. I believe that these questions are the answers and when we stop, pause and reflect, we gain a greater perspective on everything.

So, I asked myself these 5 powerful questions and I urge you to ask yourself the same whenever you're unsure of your next move:

Integrity Question: Am I being honest with myself... Really?

Legacy Question: What story do I want to tell?

Conscience Question: Is there a tension that deserves my attention?

Maturity Question: What is the wise thing to do?

Relationship Question: What does love require of me?

When I reflected on this, the biggest question I then asked myself was:

Will it be this year? Am I going to finally break the cycle once and for all?

All these powerful questions put everything back into perspective for me and it always takes me back to 10 years ago when I created a vision for how I want to live and who I want to be, affirming:

> "I am rediscovering myself every day so that I now move forward without resistance and fear about who I can be and without the need to gain permission from anyone. It is beautiful when I take that step without

thinking about who's child, partner or mother I am.

I am who I am destined to be."

Why shouldn't we step into the power of who we are destined to be? Life is for living. If you wake up every day and feel dissatisfied with the work or contribution that you are making to life, then you don't have to continue that road. If you are ready to stop being overwhelmed, underpaid, undervalued, then it's time to step forward and give yourself permission to do yourself justice.

I've finally gotten out of my own way and claimed what I actually want to do with my life. I've taken my resilience super power and everything else within my three decades of self-discovery, experience and breaking my own repeating cycles, to finally do what feels like my life work and live a life for me.

There is no going back now and there's absolutely nowhere to hide now. I live through my own challenges, experiences, soul calling, vision and wisdom that it's important not to just say it but become the voice, leader and cycle breaker - not just for myself but for those who I now get to support throughout their own transformational breakthroughs by guiding them through my JUSTICE framework, which I now use at the core of everything I teach and advise. This stands for:

JOURNEY

Your journey so far has been filled with so many lessons. How do you want to view these experiences moving forward? Whether good or bad, you can now take the learning and explore, experiment, reflect and use what you find to shape your future destination or life purpose.

UNDERSTANDING

Are you ready to make sense of how everything fits together in your life, career or business?

You can now use the knowledge that you gain, and the wisdom that you find, to create something different.

STRATEGY

Having a framework that helps you to define your vision, mission, and direction allows you the ability to adapt to change, plan and look ahead, for what you would like to happen next.

TRUTH

Embark on your transformational process by getting super specific and extremely truthful about what you'd like to achieve and the impact you would like to make.

IDENTITY

Rediscover your identity and explore your valuable qualities, personality and how you express yourself in the world by feeling confident in your individuality, self-image and self-esteem.

CLARITY

Having a focus and clear state of mind helps you to understand yourself better. No more indecisions over-whelm, or worry, enabling you to put your vision into action and appreciate your life more.

EXPANSION

Are you ready for bigger things? Are you willing to make a bigger impact in the world?

What would a bigger impact look like to you? Is it something you do for yourself or for your family, what about for your community or the world? You get to decide.

For me, to really live by my core values which I shared with you at the beginning of this chapter, for me to be able to leave a legacy in the way I desire, I have to lead by example and show what's possible so that others can be empowered to do the same, regardless of their age, gender, race or circumstance.

Many of the clients I now get to work with come to me when they are at a stage in their life where they already feel the need for change. Since 2020, the number has multiplied and very often, those who I work with are discovering that they are in the wrong job or have lost the passion for the business they created, but somehow, they feel they must continue to work on in the same situation, due to financial or family reasons - even if it is apparent that thing aren't working out their way.

The work I do now allows me to harness my skills as a Money Breakthrough & Life Transformation Coach, specialising in empowering women to start conversations that will unravel their money stories, establishing what is holding them back when it comes to their relationship with money. I can then help create new pathways to help my clients step into owning their self-worth so that they can unapologetically increase their net worth.

Always remember, you have already been gifted with everything you need to start the journey and there's no better time than NOW! So, I'm inviting you and giving YOU permission to do yourself justice.

Will it be this year for YOU?

Let's connect! You can find me at:

Website: www.BeverleyFray.com

LinkedIn:- https://www.linkedin.com/in/beverleyfray

ABOUT THE AUTHOR

BEVERLEY FRAY

Beverley Fray, a Money Breakthrough & Life Transformation Coach, helps career and business women to overcome self-doubt. By creating strategies and a new pathway to owning their self-worth, they can unapologetically increase their net worth and live a life that is truly aligned to their values, mission and purpose.

Her 30+ years of expertise came from careers in banking and finance in the UK. It has also spanned the corporate, private and the not-for-profit sectors, leading her from broking and underwriting, to advising and advocacy, through to now, coaching and mentoring.

Beverley is on a mission to get women talking about money because she believes that it's NOT just about the money, but 100% to do with how women holistically view themselves and how ready they are to also deep-dive into navigating change to create something far greater than they ever thought possible.

She has a passion for cooking and finds it a wonderful pastime for conversation, engagement, connection and relaxation. She also finds Salsa dancing and being on a beach anywhere in the world nourishing for her soul and very different to her time-gifting work of consultancy and leadership with schools, community groups and charities.

To find more of what you are looking for you can connect with Beverley on LinkedIn or at www. beverleyfray.com

Connect via the socials:

facebook.com/profile.php?id=100009016907009

instagram.com/beverleyfray

BRENDA GABRIEL

PERMISSION TO BE A REALITY STAR (EVEN IF YOU HAVE NO DESIRE TO BE ON TV)

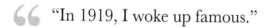

66 "In 1919, I woke up famous."

— COCO CHANEL

*A*nd seemingly out of nowhere, one year after purchasing the famous building at 31 rue Cambon, Paris, Chanel was indeed famous. Although there was no such thing as reality TV when Chanel started out, I'm quite sure her story she would have made great television.

As wonderful as Coco was and her legacy is, this isn't about her. 'It's not even about me. This is about you and allowing yourself to become a Reality Star, your way. And yes, I do appreciate that you may have no desire at all to be famous-famous. That's fine, but you don't get off the hook that easily. If you are a business owner, you actually do want to be known to the right people.

Fame and celebrity are often used interchangeably and whilst they are sisters, they are not twins. Being famous is having a reputation, or being well known in society for a specific reason, being a celebrity is about commanding media attention.

Fame is 'Big and VISIBLE personal success,' as quoted in the book, Fame 101. People tend to freak out at the mention of fame and celebrity, but anyone who has a desire for greater visibility and notoriety has a desire for fame.

Now, I'm willing to bet that you don't really have a problem with people becoming aware of your existence based on your work or contribution. After all, for you to help people, they need to be able to find you, right?

As for celebrity, its success is based on an ability to maintain social relevance. Without relevance, there's no celebrity status. The Media plays a large role in keeping someone in the public gaze. When it comes to developing a strong personality brand, both fame and celebrity are important.

I can't tell you how many people I've met during my career who tell me they have no interest in fame and celebrity, yet spend time watching or reading about or buying from notable people EVERY SINGLE DAY.

What makes them any more noteworthy than you?

I'll tell you what…

Absolutely nothing.

The truth is, as transformation providers, we ALL want to be famous with the right people for our work … Just on our terms. I'm here to let you know, it's totally possible for you.

So, who am I? We'll get to that. First, I'd like to share something with you.

If you were to unpick the stitching of the couture success suit of any entrepreneur you deem successful, somewhere in their armoire you'll find four things that underpin their success.

- A desire to do, have and BE more;
- At least one mentor or guide who helped them perceive themselves differently;
- The realisation that they weren't lazy, stupid or crazy;
- A little bit of luck.

My 'success' suit is no different and neither will yours be. Success is a funny word because it gives the impression of a final destination. A place where things are just so, a bit like the end of a Hollywood movie. Only there is no "Fin" sign when we achieve what others would call success. There is no destination, only the journey, with a series of stops along the way.

I'm co-writing this book as a seemingly successful entrepreneur with a few traditionally celebrated milestones under my Gucci belt: Eight years running my own business, my first £5k, my first five-figure month and figure year in 2018. I've appeared on TV, had an article on Huffpost, am a contributor to Thrive Global and have been quoted in Forbes. I now have a small team; my boyfriend has quit his key work job to join my business as the Operations Manager.

At the time of writing this chapter, I recently celebrated a 'yes' from a new prospect which, upon signing, will have resulted in my first ever 6-figure sales month and my highest cash month to date. I treated myself to a brand new YSL Sac de Jour handbag to celebrate.

Subsequently, due to circumstances beyond both of our control, the official celebration will have to go on hold. Whilst the rule is not to celebrate until the contract is signed and money is in the bank, I'm proud to have celebrated (a little prematurely) the fact that I, 'Benefits-Brenda', could get to a place in my business where this was even a possibility for me.

Such is the nature of success.

Contrary to popular erroneous belief and the desire for otherwise, success isn't an upward trajectory. Just as soon as there's an up, there may be a down not too far around the corner. Over time, I've learnt that success is definitely a mode of travel rather than a destination.

As for the day-to-day, I have a cleaner, I can afford to do our weekly shop at M&S, I pay my mum to do my ironing and one of my besties to help with childcare. I love being able to pay people I love in spite of the fact, I know they would help for free. I've hired a PR assistant, an OBM and a publicist to help with business growth. Whilst not quite retiring my partner, I have been able to offer him a job as my operations manager. Writing this out seems slightly surreal.

It's been some time since I've felt my face flush, worried that my debit card might be declined at the checkout because I've run out of money. Now if it's declined, it's because I've used the wrong card. When you started your adult life as a teen mum living on £70 per week in a small council flat, being able to shop in M&S and not hold your breath when making a card payment is success.

The successes I am most proud of as a result of my business have more to do with what my clients have achieved and what I've been able to do with the money made, as opposed to my personal achievements and the noughts in my bank account, such as:

The writing coach and bestselling author who hadn't sold anything for two years. Within five weeks of working together, she had made £5000 in sales for her retreat, started making book sales again and was able to travel to New York to see her son.

The publicist, who jumped from £8000 months in her PR business to making over £40,000 in sales in just five weeks. Who, by the end of the year, was able to pay herself a huge bonus and could afford the wedding of her dreams

Perhaps one of my favourite transformations was that of a lady who left the job she hated, with no back up, jumped into my boot camp and made her first ever sale. She recently just moved into a lovely flat, afforded by the increase in income made on her own terms.

I've just secured one of my clients her own reality TV show with a major production company. I secured another client a spot on the judging panel for a national awards ceremony. My clients have appeared on TV, have been in some of the biggest publications and, in some instances, have gone viral.

I love being my own boss, but more than that, I love having a sense of purpose that drives me, daily.

I've come a long way since I started my business, yet it feels weird to use the word successful to describe myself. I still have so much to achieve.

Allow me to introduce myself. I'm Brenda, a self-styled Fame PR Queen. So called because I'm on a mission to create a new breed of celebrity.

Conscious Celebrity.

I live to raise the profile of purpose driven, convention breaking entrepreneurs with a powerful story and a message the world needs to hear. Pioneers, who desire to become the maverick celebrity who leverages their authority, influence and fame to effect massive, positive impact on a global scale.

Sounds pretty grand, even to me. To coin a cliché, life wasn't always like this. In fact, it was a twist of fate that led to me searching for my something more. In July 2012- I was run off my bicycle by a van en-route to my fitness boot camp before work.

As I lay on the floor, dazed and high on adrenaline, after the initial thought of "FFS! I'm going to miss boot camp", my second thought was "I could have died a civil servant!"

Unable to do much more than shiver, I knew after months of wishing I could just stop doing the job that didn't my set soul on fire, I believe I had inadvertently called in the accident to force me to do something about it. Luckily, I suffered no more than a jarred back and a few scars. One month later I discovered I was pregnant.

Seven months after that, the opportunity to take volunteered paid redundancy came up. Me and my eight-month pregnant belly jumped at the opportunity. Despite my successes and career progression, I severely lacked confidence in my ability and suffered massively from imposter syndrome. Not at all helped by the fact that I was often ignored in team meetings and struggled to fit in. I thought I was imagining it until my bestie stood up for me in a meeting when the suggestion I had just put forward, was ignored. Once it had been repeated verbatim by a male manager, amazingly, everyone heard him and congratulated him on such a brilliant idea.

I was always questioning why things were done the way they were. It was apparent to me the way things were being done wasn't the most effective! It never occurred to me that if things did work, many people would probably be out of a job. #NoShade.

When I think back to how unhappy I was, for so long, for the sake of a salary, it saddens me. I believed that "not that bad" was interchangeable with "good".

It wasn't until years after I left that job, I realised that being ignored in meetings was something that numerous women experienced in the work place.

Even when I was diagnosed with depression and anxiety, brought on in part by unhappiness in the job, I thought the problem was me. At the time I was I was responsible for advising teams on implementing and running an 'optimum business model'. Pretty quickly, I realised most units were running a one-legged race and didn't have the resources to operate effectively. Rather than give them the resource required, my job was to mark them down for failing to achieve an impossible standard.

But then, no-one was supposed to love their job, were they? Work was a means to an end. I earned a good salary, had 6 weeks paid holiday a year, childcare vouchers, a final salary pension and if I kept my head down, I'd have a job for life. What more did I want?

A lot, it seemed.

We all know when a situation isn't right for us. It feels uncomfortable, and not in a stretching out of your comfort zone way. It feels more like a soul suck. We stick it out because we believe we 'should'. That it's lazy, stupid or crazy not to.

If you find yourself feeling this way, if I could give you one piece of advice it would be this... Don't ignore your gut/heart/intuition when it tells you that something isn't right, no matter how great things appear to be on the surface. And don't sit around waiting for it to get better if things show no sign of getting better and you have no intention of changing anything. One thing I've learned in life is that nothing changes if we don't. Rarely, if ever, do things improve without us making a concerted effort to change who we are in the situation. If anything, when we choose to remain in a bad situation things almost always get worse.

If I'm honest, I knew I was unhappy in my job two positions before it. In 2009, I spent two years making up my own job role because of a misunderstanding which found me surplus to requirements as an Executive Assistant. My saving grace was I met my partner shortly after getting the job, which meant when I wasn't making myself busy, I could spend time getting to know him on the phone.

Also, don't be afraid to speak up when people infringe your boundaries. I was terrible at speaking up for myself. I was a brilliant advocate for others, always have been, but when it came to standing up for myself, I hated confrontation and had a fear of authority. Back then, I considered myself lucky for having a job for life with great benefits when so many others didn't. It didn't make sense to rock the boat - after all, it's not like anyone was actually mean to me - because I had such low boundaries and standards.

My mum always used to say her mum told her "If it doesn't have horns, no need to fear it". I wish I had lived by that motto as a young woman. It's taken me years to realise that mastering difficult conversations is key to banishing fear of confrontation. That's what I've chosen to take from that saying.

As for leaving my job, it was a relief when I received the letter to say I would be released.

Weeks away from giving birth, I had no plan. Initially I thought I was going to make my money selling hair extensions. I also joined a network marketing model for an energy company and invested the compensation from my accident into a property course. Half way through the course I realised that I didn't have the contacts, resources or chutzpa to start buying properties at below market value. What did excite me however, was the marketing and PR segment, where I had my eyes open to the power of marketing and PR.

After absorbing what I could over two days, I decided that I wanted to be a marketer.

Within a matter of weeks, I'd arranged a preliminary meeting with the founder of a top London PR company, Jessica Huie, MBE, to talk about taking over her social media marketing. My bestie knew Jessica well and put in a good word for me (remember what I said about luck?). I managed to convince Jessica that I would be able to get her on the front page of google with the skills I'd learned on my course. Jessica gave me 24 hours to put together a proposal.

It took me a whole day to pull one together but I did it. She decided to give a me a chance, working two days a week. Within a few weeks, her website ranked No. 1 for several search terms. Though I knew I could do it, I had no idea of the how. I was so determined to make it work, there was no option for it to go any other way. During the time I worked at JHPR, I started to learn about PR and was given the opportunity to write press releases, create media lists and help on accounts.

The agency won the contract for the government initiative, Start Up Loans, and were tasked with the PR for their awards. I was given the responsibility of getting PR for some of the winners, which I absolutely loved. It was a great feeling to see the coverage I had got for the startups appear in print.

At the time I was with JHPR, their roster included the likes of Meghan Markle, Richard Branson and Sir Bob Geldof. Hearing Jessica talk about the close relationships she had with certain celebs and some of the interviews she had done made me want to work with celebs. I never realised at the time, I would want to create them.

After a few months, it was time to move on. I discovered a month or so later that I was pregnant with my daughter. Due to a non-compete clause in my contract, rather than continue my love affair with PR, I decided to go into social media marketing.

I went from a stable salary to earning hundreds of pounds as a social media marketing strategist. At one point, I was sharing a £350 pound account with one of my besties. My income was so low I had to apply for a £9 per hour call centre job. I didn't last long due to residual back pain from being run over, so I had to go onto benefits - a real low point after paying my way since the age of 18.

After taking five months maternity leave, I hired my first business coach. She was my biggest cheerleader at the time and quickly helped me double my income from £400 to £800 per month.

My next mentor continued to push me out of my comfort zone and convinced me to go back to my first love of PR. I didn't make a single PR sale during that time, but I did set up my first monthly mastermind which I was super proud of.

2017 was when things really transformed for me. Before, we get to the good part, I feel it's only right to talk about why I felt the need to avoid doing things my way.

Although you're unlikely to be able to tell from my neutral accent, I grew up in the small town called Huddersfield. My mum moved there with her family when she came over to the UK at 18 where she met my dad, who had given up an electrician job in the BBC to move to Huddersfield where the house prices were more reasonable.

I was born in 1981 to unemployed parents in Thatcher's Britain. My mum never finished school in the Caribbean as she was needed at home. My father also never finished school due to being expelled when he retaliated after someone tried to bully him.

In spite of this, he was one of the most intelligent people I will ever meet. He was a computer and electronics nerd and would code programs and games for us on his Commadore +4. Although we were poor and were dressed in clothes from local charity shops, we were surrounded by gadgets and computers.

We never received Christmas presents apart from one year where my dad bought me a life-size Effie doll.

Sadly, that doll caused a huge row between my parents, which I heard when I sneaked down the stairs to listen. My present meant we didn't have enough money for a Christmas spread and mum was understandably furious.

For most of my life, that experience led me to believe I could only prosper at the expense of someone else. My default became 'either/or'. Today, I realise that my dad chose me. He chose my joy on Christmas Day over a standard Christmas for them. He made that choice because he believed I was worth it.

Knowing that money was difficult for us to come by, affected me deeply. So much so, that I based my career option on the fact that 'people like me' didn't become barristers.

I was a very bright, academic student, who gave up in my dream of becoming a barrister at the age of 12 once I saw how much it would cost just to buy a wig and gown and couldn't see how I would afford to put myself through training without working. I decided I would go into business management instead. It never even occurred to me to find out how I could make it happen. The cost for me was a dead end.

I lacked confidence as a child. Next to my dad, I felt stupid. He would explain concepts that I didn't understand at the time and would often get frustrated that my 6-year-old brain couldn't run with the adult concepts he was throwing down.

My parents were also very strict, so talking back wasn't something they tolerated. Unwittingly, this led to me not speaking up for myself, which was a habit I carried into adulthood.

My self-talk as a teen and young adult was pretty poor. When it came to work, I was always afraid of being found out. I never really felt like I knew what I was doing in any scenario. I'd tell myself I wasn't qualified enough for the job I was doing and be convinced I should be doing a better job.

I literally picked myself apart in the same way I felt my parents did. My attitude towards my physical appearance wasn't much better. Nine years ago, I was at the peak of my fitness. I was down to 22% body fat, had a resting pulse of 45 beats per minute and could run a 7-minute mile. I was in the best shape of my life but instead of celebrating that I was still finding fault with the fact my stomach was flat rather than concaved, the way it was in my teens.

A lot of what my dad taught me as a child has stayed with me. I just didn't understand the value of what he was sharing at the time. Deep down I've always known that there is always a better, faster, easier way to do most things. My dad used to use basic circuits to teach me that the fastest way from A-B was a straight line. He applied this logic to everything in life. He'd tell me to be direct and go straight for what I wanted.

In every job, I seemed to be surrounded by people who seemed to enjoy taking the scenic route.

The think is, this doesn't just happen in the corporate world. It happens in the entrepreneurial world too. I know because I was guilty of it. One of the most valuable lessons I've learned is the fact that strategy is the fastest way from A-B for the individual.

What do I mean by that? I mean that there is no such thing as a cookie cutter strategy because what works for someone else won't work exactly the same way for you. This applies to almost everything.

I spent so much time at the start of my journey, implementing strategies that didn't work for me, 'working my way up' to success because I was told by the experts that I couldn't go straight for what I wanted. I needed to take a stepping stone approach to success.

PR was a good example of this. Many PR experts would talk about the need to pitch multiple outlets daily in the hope of getting a bite. I always found I had better results when I later focused on one outlet, one journalist and focused on tailoring the pitch for an audience of one. In the first instance it took longer but it meant I got results a lot faster.

Using this strategy, I'm able to secure coveted pieces of coverage and opportunities for my clients with ease. Like the time I got one client to go viral in the Daily Mail in a matter of weeks, resulting in an invitation to Good Morning Britain and the offer of a reality TV show.

Another client went viral with her first article in Elephant Journal after I suggested she turn her social media post into an article.

Another client secured over 40 global pieces of syndicated coverage from one well-placed article in the Daily Mail.

Fast forward to today and, less than a month into our engagement, I secured another client an interview with an award-winning production company. The pilot is set to be filmed in September 2021.

As I said, getting to this place was a journey. Although I knew there was always an alternative way to the status quo that would work better for me, it took some time for me to trust my intuition. Despite having taken a huge first step by leaving my job, I wasn't entirely able to embrace MY way of doing things for a while yet.

I really wish I could say nearly losing my life was enough to shake me into doing everything my way from that day forward, but it wasn't. The programming that stops many of us from fully submitting to our inner guide, runs deep. That said, I'm a strong believer that things unfold as they should. If nothing else our journey, including its downs, is what adds gravitas and value to expertise.

If I'm honest, even up until joining the mastermind behind this book, there were still areas in my business and my life where I wasn't fully leaning into doing things my way.

Case in point, it took me three years after starting my online business to market myself as a publicist. I touted myself out as a social media manager, partly because I signed a non-compete clause with the PR agency where I honed my craft and partly because, as a relative beginner, I was scared to charge the sort of money I would need to as a publicist.

As a result, I ended up doing some enjoyable but not very well-paid gigs, securing the odd bit of press coverage, which in hindsight, probably worked well because juggling two under 5-year-olds, with a partner who travelled a lot for work, while building a business was no small task.

One day, my mentor at the time told me it sounded like the work I was doing and wanted to do was in PR. I agreed. That day Brenda Gabriel PR was born, but rather than successfully selling PR, I somehow ended up selling a business mastermind and offering high value branding photo shoots - which didn't sell.

At the time I blamed my lack of sales on the fact that either clients weren't interested in Fame/Personal Branding, or they didn't see the value in being famous or looking the part to raise their profile. At no point did I think to question the methods I was using to attract clients, or the fact that I wasn't able to articulate the value of publicity.

The other factor that held me back from success was I had no sense of self when it came to business. I downloaded Megabytes of freebies from multiple coaches and took advice from anyone who was giving it. I'd try to adjust my methods to whatever was in vogue at the time, rather than accepting there were some things that just weren't for me - such as selling low end, or super high end when I didn't have either the tools, business structure, knowledge or confidence to implement at either scale.

I now charge more for PR services than I was told to charge four years ago. Whereas I'm fully aware of the value I can provide, back then I had no clue. Little wonder I couldn't sell one package at that price.

I never knew how to differentiate between what worked for others and what would work for me.

It didn't matter how great I was at securing coverage if I struggled to help my audience understand why they should care and invest nor understand what people who would invest in PR actually wanted to buy. I'll give you a clue... It wasn't press coverage. It took me another year to realise that people didn't want coverage. They wanted the result of that coverage. They wanted to know what being in a certain publication would mean for them and their business. Honestly, at the time, I wasn't bold enough to state that I could help them become famous because although I had worked in an agency that worked with established celebs, turning an unknown into a celebrity wasn't something I had ever done. I knew the ingredients required and I knew how to bake, I just hadn't baked a Fame cake from start to finish yet and that stopped me from offering the cake, even at a lower price point.

In 2017, I secured my first six-month PR client, and then another, and another. I started securing great features with ease. One lady ended up on the Victoria Derbyshire show to talk about her book. Another lady was invited to contribute to a platform set up by Michelle Mone. A couple of clients went viral and things really took off from there.

Instead of asking myself how I was going to get amazing results, I put my desire to get amazing results front and centre, and changed the question to what would I need to do to get the results. A small shift, but significant in terms of going from doing the thing, to BEing the thing that made all things happen. It may sound a bit woo, but the truth as I know it is that belief is stronger than almost any circumstance. I hired clients I believed deserved to be famous through PR and they started to gain traction.

If you ever find yourself feeling doubtful about your ability to do the thing you were born to, you might want to do something similar and ask yourself who would you BE if you knew you could achieve the outcome you desire.

Letting go of old narratives that no longer served me, especially in relation to how I perceived myself, definitely had the biggest impact on my success. At the time, I thought it was purely my relationship to money but it was so much more than that. It's also precisely why my process to build a personal profile or increase income starts with shifting internal perception. Once that's taken care of, the way someone is perceived externally naturally shifts to match the 'vibration' of what's going on internally. This is why my clients find that an increase in income and opportunities to be more visible is a standard side effect of our work together.

I suppose you could say, learning to give myself permission to be the star of my own reality TV show has been, and still is, an ongoing journey. There's always room for improvement. I've learned that doing it my way can look different from one day to the next. One day it's being brash and bold on social media or putting myself forward for PR opportunities, other times it involves living fame vicariously through my amazing clients as they become more and more well-known (with the odd bit of time out to internet window shop :)).

"How many cares one loses when once decides not to be something but to be someone."

— COCO CHANEL

Another favourite Chanel quote that is most apt for me. Once I stopped trying to be an 'Entrepreneur', 'Sales coach', 'Publicist' or 'Consultant', I was able to focus on who I wanted to BE. I stopped worrying about my niche and became one.

I wanted to be the person who helped emerging celebrities get 'Fame ready' in every way, from having a website that speaks to the media, to improving their business model, to getting a media mindset. I wanted to be the person who helped disruptors make their valuable contribution to society and build a legacy through valuable relationships and leveraging the media.

To my mind, there is no other strategy that has the potential to change, not just the life of a change maker and the people who've had the privilege to work with them, but also those they may never meet, who may be inspired to take action just because they came across them sharing their story. Not advertising, not marketing, not even a launch because the only people who benefit are those who already have an interest in buying.

What about those who don't even know they need your transformational service or that it exists? How is it possible to connect with them if you don't leverage the media?

Outside of that, my clients have found that connecting with the right clients can change the entire trajectory of their business. Often the type of client they want to connect with isn't on Facebook or IG. Especially when it comes to celebs and High Net Worth Individuals the only way to connect with them is to be in the places they hang out. They also need to perceive you as an authority. This usually happens in two ways - an introduction or encountering you in a place where your positioning demonstrates you are the right fit for them.

No amount of Facebook ads or funnels will ever get Jennifer Anniston or J-Lo as your client. I said just as much to one of my first PR retainer clients. That line was enough to close the deal because she knew it was true - having spent thousands on Facebook ads prior. As it turns out we did reach out to Jennifer Anniston's people and they did respond with interest in my client's services. I can't say anything more than that but you don't need me to tell you we could have never have got that result via a Facebook ad.

ITS ALL ABOUT PEOPLE when it comes to PR. Money is just a happy side effect. No one actually needs PR to make money, but how much are things likely to change in your business once you get referrals from A-List clients? When you're able to take a selfie with said A-Lister, not because you paid for a meet and greet but because you helped changed their life? That is how you begin to leave a global impact. Your network alone will grow insane value, over and above any financial reward.

There's a world of difference between being a real-world industry insider and online fame. Global influence and impact doesn't stay online. Celebrity is an art.

It requires dedication to your craft and an ability to make it about your audience rather than you. Being able to speak to your soul audience whilst remaining relative to the masses is a talent in itself. I tell my clients; it's not about just connecting them with celebrities. I want them to become celebrated for their transformational work.

Fame and celebrity aren't for everyone, which is why I've spent the past few years developing a method of PR that helps clients develop emotional stability for life as an emerging public figure. Jay-Z's 'Holy Grail' touches upon the love/hate relationship celebs have with fame. Most, if not all, will deal with some degree of trolling or other challenges associated with life in the public eye. I wanted to make sure I was in a position to equip clients with the tools to navigate this. In fact, in my opinion the best way to deal with impostor syndrome is to increase your visibility and learn to see yourself the way your audience does.

Though every win is a celebration, it's how the lives of my clients and me have changed as result of this work that means the most to me:

Like the client whose Daily Mail feature resulted in Good Morning Britain reaching out and her first national TV segment, which lasted 20 minutes. Not to mention the global interest from as far afield as New Zealand. She also had her first 100k month a few months into working together, and a few months after we stopped working together hit 7 figures in her business.

Another client went viral in Elephant Journal with a Facebook post I suggested she submit as an article. This got over 30,000 views and 6000 shares in a matter of weeks.

There's the client who credited the work we did for taking her from inconsistent £5k months and a desire to have a 6-figure year, to having a £54k month. And she is still going from strength to strength. More importantly, she took full ownership of her work and, despite never having been in the media, is an online celebrity in her niche. The outcome that made me smile the most was the fact she was able to visit her family abroad and not worry about how much she was spending.

Or the client who accidentally hit a £25k month after trying to crack a £20k month, then realised she had made six-figures in the first four months of the year. More importantly, she was able to give up the things that didn't give her joy, semi-retire her husband, move country and set up a life in the sun.

Or the client who fell pregnant shortly after our work together showed her she was totally capable of manifesting what she desired.

And the list goes on.

All because I stopped worrying about the what and the how and focused on being the person who could achieve those results.

So, to end, let me share with you this. There is no ONE way for you to have success. There is only YOUR way. And this way can change depending on your season, circumstance AND personality type. As a mum of three, semi-traditional in my views on relationships, an introvert and someone who prefers quality over quantity...

I never wanted to hand over the household reigns to my partner. I enjoy private work because I value string relationships and intimacy. I didn't want to be hands off in my business; I wanted to sell high-value and I wanted to share my energy with the RIGHT people, not lots of people.

When I started my business, the online world told me these desires were pie in the sky.

The gurus didn't make money that way. I struggled for years trying to fit my star shaped self into a round 'entrepreneurial' hole.

Eventually, I found the mentor who backed the way I desired to make money.

Since then, I've vacillated between doing things my way, and thinking and worrying that I need to do 'something' different, to proof my business, cos the gravy train might stop and it all might end.

I invested in a second business, new programs and courses, many of which were either not used or weren't right for me at the time because of the energy from which I invested.

I have not been immune from taking action or investing from desperate energy. No surprise then, when I couldn't make money from that space.

I got behind with payments. The harder I worked, the less I achieved. The past couple of months, mountains have shifted while I've operated from flow.

This does NOT mean I sat back and emitted glitter rainbow unicorn frequency from my 'gina. I still worked for it, slept too few hours, gained weight, didn't speak to friends, put work before housework, but it FELT right. It was no longer a struggle.

If I put the work in, things just worked. There's a belief that if we operate from flow, we don't have to work. That may be the case for some, but not for me.

Everything I have achieved, AM achieving, I worked for. Every counterintuitive decision, like borrowing money to invest when I couldn't pay current obligations, I fully owned, KNOWING that it needed to be done that way.

MY way. And it paid off.

I've finally hit the tipping point where it feels like money is being thrown at me to work magic.

And although I created this without funnels and all the other things I was told I needed, that doesn't mean I'm not ready to scale up with all the things I didn't require in my building phase.

One reason I hired my partner to come on board was to implement the funnels I know I need to scale what I've created. It may appear like overnight success, or just another rags to riches tale, but please know that for me it has been eight years in the making, with numerous F Ups, upsets, two babies, two miscarriages, coming close to giving up when the world got to me and I made no money for four months last year, and countless tears to get here.

There is no ONE way, there is only YOUR way.

So, reintroduce you to yourself, then to the world, without your mask and unapologetically - your audience is waiting to discover it's YOU they've been missing all along.

You'll piss some people off, but keep going.

You'll trigger old wounds, keep going.

You'll question your sanity, keep going.

You may feel like giving up completely, keep going.

When you get to the other side, you'll understand why it had to be that way and you'll never take it for granted.

I promise.

ABOUT THE AUTHOR

BRENDA GABRIEL

Brenda Gabriel, the self-styled Fame PR Queen and Creator of the Conscious Celebrity PR Method, is a Publicist and Premium Sales Strategist who helps convention-breaking founders and influencers attain global industry fame through targeted PR and publicity campaigns.

Prior to setting up her business, Brenda spent 11 years in the Civil Service. After five years in project implementation and communications, then a stint in a top London PR agency with a client roster including the likes of Meghan Markle, Sir Bob Geldof and Sir Richard Branson, Brenda helped start up business founders raise their profile and increase brand awareness through digital media and publicity.

Brenda has secured her clients national and global features in prominent media such as the BBC, Forbes, Harper's Bazaar, and the Daily Mail, which has led to expert TV appearances, viral press coverage, TED X invites and reality TV opportunities.

Brenda now consults emerging public figures on corporate messaging, positioning, securing broadcast and top-tier press coverage, in addition to brand and celeb collaborations.

When not working to elevate insanely talented experts to rockstar celebrity status, Brenda can be found at the gym, travelling or indulging her penchant for fine dining and champagne.

Brenda lives in London, UK, with her partner Brad and their three children.

Brenda is available for PR engagements and private consultations on how to leverage publicity to increase revenue and opportunities.

You can reach Brenda at:

Email - <u>*brenda@brendagabriel.co.uk*</u>

Website - <u>*www.brendagabriel.co.uk*</u>

 facebook.com/brendagabriel

 instagram.com/FamePRQueen

PERMISSION TO GET OUTSIDE YOUR COMFORT ZONE AND GROW YOUR BUSINESS ORGANICALLY.

*W*ell paid hippie...that is what my brother once referred to me as. My family have no idea what I do, they just know I sit on social media and get paid pretty well for it. I don't blame them at all… I do sit on social media and get paid pretty well for it.

I designed my business around the life I wanted to lead; travel and life first, business second. That means: I don't book client calls in on Mondays or Fridays; I only work with people that have missions that excite me; oh, and to date I haven't paid any of the social media giants any money in ads to get in front of my audience.

In 2019, the year in which we were allowed to travel, I traveled to eight different countries and increased turnover in my business by 138% on the previous year! All without ads and just putting in place completely unique strategies to attract my clients. I will explain more about these strategies later on in this chapter.

In 2020, I realised that the strategies I was using inside of my Social Media Marketing Agency were not being used or taught in the way I was doing it, and I knew there were other service based entrepreneurs that needed to know how to generate clients easier. So, I transitioned to coaching, to help those service based entrepreneurs do exactly the same thing I had done, and 2021 saw me hitting the £10k+ per month milestone consistently in my business.

But it wasn't always roses, unicorns and £10k months.

When I finished university, I was living the life that I thought I should. You know, the one where you are told to get a good job, get married and settle down. I had just got the job of my dreams as a wedding planner, and I was living with my boyfriend but it wasn't all it was cracked up to be.

The boyfriend finished with me and I spent the hour and half commute to work every day crying. I even put my makeup on when I got to work so I didn't smudge my mascara with tears.

New Years Eve 2012, the clock struck midnight and I looked around at the party scene that surrounded me and I realised that this wasn't the life I wanted.

The next day, I applied for a job in Thailand teaching English, and in April I sold everything I owned! I mean everything.

I was driving to work on the last day of work and my car started making a strange noise. I pulled into the mechanics and asked them to look at it. They came back to me and said you can't drive this anywhere, the engine is about to go. I took one look at the man and burst into tears. The poor mechanic looked at me with a look of sheer panic and, in true English manner, asked me if I wanted a cup of tea.

I was driving to work that day and selling the car that night. My flight to Thailand was two days later and all the money I was taking with me was the price I was getting for that car.

I phoned the dealer buying the car and explained the situation. They said they would still buy the car but that they would reduce the price by £1000. The recovery driver came to pick me and the car up from the garage to tow me to the dealer and as we sat in the cab, I told him my story. He looked at me and said "You are so brave. I don't know if I could sell everything and leave."

I burst into tears again… "Brave??? Are you kidding? I am F**king Stupid! That is what I am!" The recovery driver didn't say a word the rest of the way home.

Why am I telling you this story? Because this was one of the biggest and scariest moments in my life and by just saying "I got on a plane" makes it sound like this was an easy thing for me to do. It absolutely was not easy and there are hundreds of more moments in my story during which I could have given up and said never mind, but I am always reminded that nothing good ever comes from inside of your comfort zone, and pushing yourself regardless of the obstacles is the only way you get "lucky".

It was during this time in Thailand that I realised that I wasn't meant for teaching children, mainly because I wasn't a fan of them. I also realised that I 100% did not want to go back to a 3-hour commute in a minimum wage job. I had to find another way that fit into the lifestyle I wanted to create for myself, and so the work began and the journey continued.

I struggled a lot! I took a course, then another course, then a webinar and someone else's challenge. I played around on Facebook and tried to learn everything I could. I freelanced whilst working jobs, as I was living in Australia by then. This went on for four years. I had no idea what I wanted to do or how to do it, but I was determined to try to make this work. Eventually I realised that if I was going to make this work, I couldn't stay in Australia because of the visa situation and I needed to be somewhere else in the world. So, I did, it again, I got out of my comfort zone, I sold everything and moved countries.

Nothing good comes from inside of your comfort zone. If you are feeling stuck, or like something isn't right in your life. I highly recommend making a dramatic change. The more dramatic the change the less chance you have of going back to what seems comfortable for you. Don't settle for what you think is the life that you "should" want; strive for the live you actually want. Get outside of your comfort zone and don't give yourself a safety net.

I went into my boss's office and asked for a word. I told her that I wanted to hand in my notice and that I was extremely grateful for the opportunity of being sponsored, but I needed to do this. She said "You are 30 years old do you really think you should be living in hostels with no money again? You should take two weeks and make sure this decision is really what you want." Needless to say, my answer was the same when I came back two weeks later.

I sold everything once again and booked a one way flight to Bali, to figure out how to make this business thing a success. I secured some freelance roles from upwork and started building out what I thought my brand would look like. But after eight months and countless times of looking at an empty bank account, I gave up and booked a one-way flight home. Five years of travelling, working and living abroad coming to an end because I couldn't make this business work.

I got a job in a digital marketing agency as an account manager, managing a team of amazing people that could do incredible things. I felt validated, like they knew I was good at this and wanted to pay me for it, so someone out there must also realise I am pretty good at this stuff.

So, I put my head down again in my business. Finally, I finished the website that had been under construction and pushed it live....nothing. No one came knocking on my door. Until they did.

I was driving to work one day listening to Jen Sincero - How to be a Badass at Making Money. If you haven't listened to it then I would hit download on any audible player now. BUT, be warned, it is very cheesy and full of over-the-top Americanisms. It is shouting from the top of your lungs, it is wooting and waving your arms in the air over the top! But, I had nothing to loose, so there I was shouting from the top of my lungs, waving my hands in the air...as I sat at the traffic lights in busy rush hour in Manchester city centre. Yes, I got some funny looks. I was screaming. "I am going to make an extra £1000 in the next 3 months."

I got out of the car and my phone beeped. I picked it up and there was a message from someone I had met three years earlier, whilst living in Sydney.

"Are you that girl that met me in a cafe to teach me hootsuite?"

Yes, yes I was THAT girl!

He responded with "Are you working for yourself?"

Yes, yes, I was.

I sent him over my sparkly new website and he responded with a screenshot of the package he wanted: £300 per month for minimum 3-month contract... Holy crap! I had just manifested the money I wanted in less than an hour of the screaming and arm throwing.

This was the kick I needed to figure out how I was going to make this business a success. No more sitting on my butt. Other people knew I was good at this and they were hiring me and paying me to do it, so it was time to commit!

I felt like clients were finding me, but they were very few and far between. I kept looking at all of these other people that had seemingly started at the same time as me and were doing so well. They seemed to be making tons of money and I was just scraping by.

There had to be something that I was doing wrong. I didn't have a strategy. I didn't have a plan. I certainly did not have a marketing ecosystem and I was just switching from one thing to another looking for the magic pill. Can you relate to this? I have messages from people all the time telling me they don't have a strategy yet and they started their businesses 10 months ago or even worse, a few years ago and they are still not making anywhere near enough money. This is when I have to be harsh and tell them that they have an expensive hobby, not a business, and without a strategy, it is going to be hard work.

I had a few clients leave me after the initial 3-month contract. I was devastated. Why was this happening to me? What was it I was doing wrong? I still had that very first client that signed up with me so why were these new ones leaving?

I realised that each of my clients were at different places in their journey and wanted different things and results. Some people thought that hiring me, a social media manager, I would literally fix every leaking hole in their pipeline and that they could just sit back and wait for the clients to roll in.

Some of the clients thought I was going to create content that was perfectly in their tone of voice and targeted at their ideal client like magic, without any consultation work at all.

I was a freebie monster... I literally downloaded everything to try to figure out why my clients were not staying and why I wasn't getting a consistent stream of clients.

This really hit me hard! I almost threw in the towel and decided maybe this entrepreneurial world wasn't really for me after all. I felt like everyone else had this nailed and I was the only one that was struggling to make it work.

I started becoming present again in my day time job because, clearly, that was what I needed to do to stay afloat. I wanted to buy a house and maybe this side hustle just wasn't going to allow for that.

Then I got moved roles at work. They realised my skill set in social media and wanted me to move into the social media department to help them increase engagement.

That was the validation I needed.

They thought I was good enough, so why didn't I believe it? They were willing to move me into a different department because they saw the skill set I had, but I couldn't see it for myself.

This changed my beliefs massively and pushed me back into action in my business.

This time, I was going to find a way that worked for me. No ads, no webinar funnels, no complicated processes - just me being me and helping people get visible, without the hustle or the overheads.

So, with my new found belief in myself, I pushed forward and... got another job! I know what you are thinking, but I still wasn't confident enough to finally go out on my own... plus I still had not got that mortgage sorted.

The job I landed meant that I was able to work from home, so no commute time and more time for building my business on the side. I thought this would be the perfect mixture.

I stepped into my power and owned my presence on social media. I was everywhere. I was in all the groups and doing all the networking. I was perfecting the system, that I now teach others to do, to secure their first clients. I was being a networking ninja.

By now, I had nailed my niche...ultimately. I wanted to work with nice people that inspired me and helped to make the world a better place. So my niche was well-ness entrepreneurs. I became known in the industry because I was always talking about wellness entrepreneurs and how they could leverage social media to scale their business, I had a growing Facebook group and a website that was full of blog content targeted at this niche. I had carved out a space for me and was building out my marketing ecosystem.

It was this strategy that saw me secure one of my biggest clients, who I worked with for the last three years. Being active in groups and being really specific with the clients that I wanted to work with allowed me to stand out and get a client from one of those "looking for a social media manager" style posts. I knew that my comments had to stand out, be specific and show that I was the expert in the industry that they were looking for. None of this "I will DM you" or "Hire me" comments, but a detailed explanation of how I could help them with case studies to back it up. That, in conjunction with the elevation content I was sharing as part of my ecosystem, secured me the role. More on the marketing ecosystem later in the chapter.

I was doing all this whilst working the full-time job from home. I want you to know that it is possible to build a profitable business whilst working full time and in fact, I would recommend it. But, be prepared for the time it takes; it is hard work and you do have to be dedicated. I was working before and after work and would even work on my lunch break too. You have to really want this, otherwise the temptation to not work will be too easy. Having created a successful business before leaving my full time job was one of the reasons I was able to make the next time I quit, the last time I quit a job.

The clients started coming in eventually. I was being giving referrals and people started recognising me as the person in the wellness industry that was going to be able to help them. I hired my first VA to help me manage the workload whilst I was working full time and I would highly recommend you also hire early! Hiring early allowed me to focus on business growth, while someone else was working on the other things that needed to be done.

But I still didn't feel confident enough to quit that stable income. I had just bought a house. I was a single women living on my own. I didn't have anyone else to fall back on. No one was going to pay the bills for me.

The boss I had at the time had a drug problem and one night, at about 1am, I got a barrage of emails from him telling me that I didn't have a job anymore. I woke up to check my emails and hit pure panic. I phoned friends, family, legal advice, anyone I could think of to give me some advice.

That afternoon, he rang as if nothing had happened - as if, everything was completely normal - with a nonchalant, "Oh sorry about that, I also sent abuse to our clients."

It was at that moment, I took the bull by the horns and finally stepped up and into my power as an entrepreneur. I wrote my resignation letter and hovered over the enter button for hours. A friend finally sat on the phone with me until I hit send. That was October 2018.

I was terrified!

I figured I could get a job if I didn't make enough money and my clients all left me. That felt safe. But, nothing good comes from inside of your comfort zone, remember?

So, I booked a one-way ferry ticket for me and my dog to drive to the south of Spain. I couldn't get a job in Spain because I didn't speak the language, so I had to make the business work to be able to afford the ferry ride home and pay the mortgage.

I hired my very first 1:1 coach when I got to Spain and I sat down with my dad to have chat about the cost and what I was about to spend on a coach. He said "Could you do it on your own?" I was pretty sure that I could do it on my own, but that would take time to figure out. I wanted to be able to sky rocket my success and not have to figure it out as I went. I wanted success now not later. If you are thinking about working with a coach then I would absolutely recommend thinking about your goals, how far do you want to go and how quickly do you want to get there? I promise you can figure it out on your own, but it will take time. If you have huge goals then invest in someone that can help you get there quicker.

I doubled my monthly salary by the time I returned from Spain in January 2019. I was feeling much more confident about my business and I now had the systems in place to help me to scale. There was no going back and getting a job now.

There was a distinct reason, I built my business the way that I did. At the time, I had no money and no confidence in myself. But in doing it this way, I found a system that worked for me.

I realised that I had the skills to be able to scale my business without having ads or traditional funnels or anything else that all those countless freebies told me that I might need. I realised that all I needed to be successful in my business was me, getting out of my comfort zone and getting out of my own way.

I built what I call a marketing ecosystem around me and you can do this too. It is a super simple concept but it is just different from what you may have heard in the past.

Traditionally you have a funnel system in which people are taken from awareness, interest, evaluation, intent, to sale at the bottom of the funnel. You may need ads, systems and expensive software in this funnel which ultimately may or may not work, depending on your offer and your ideal clients.

In a marketing ecosystem, you are allowing people to meet you exactly where they are and buy from you in a way that feels aligned with them, not in a manner that you dictate to them. There is not one singular touch-point in this system, but rather a number of different ways that you have communicated or connected with each individual. This could be through other people's Facebook groups, your personal profile, inside your Facebook group, on your email list, on your Instagram, over on LinkedIn or Pinterest... The options for your personal ecosystem are endless and ultimately it comes down to what you love doing.

You have come this far in my story so you will know by now, that I am not one for staying stuck in a situation I don't love.

If you don't love what you are doing, stop doing it and do something different.

"You are not a tree."

So, if you have been doing a LinkedIn strategy and you hate the platform then stop doing it, regardless of the guru that told you this was the perfect strategy for you. If you don't love it, your clients will know.

I personally, absolutely love Facebook Groups; I love the community, the energy and the collaboration that goes into having a Facebook group. There are so many ways you can connect and build better relationships with people, so that is where my energy and my focus has been.

The thing that makes a marketing ecosystem different to a traditional funnel is that people can bounce around and see a variety of content, information and value from you depending on the copy you are sharing at that time. Meaning that when they are ready to buy, they come knocking on your door, sliding into your DM's and being ready to work with you straight away.

When you are building a business we cannot rely solely on the platforms on which they are built. Facebook, Clickfunnels, or any other software you use could collapse at any time. An ecosystem allows you to create that all around strategy that really fits your ideal clients so that if one leg falls off, you have the others to keep you going.

People will meet you at different stages of their journey. Some might be ready to buy from you on day one of meeting you, and this has 100% happened to me. On the other side, people might hang around your marketing ecosystem for years before they are ready to buy from you. A marketing ecosystem gives both of these types of people access to you.

One thing that massively changed my business was understanding the power of positioning, what that actually meant and how I could position myself in a way that would attract clients. Ultimately, it came down to the content I was sharing and the way I was talking about myself and how I helped others.

First you need to get super clear and intentional on the things that make you different to all the others that are offering the same thing as you. Let's not kid ourselves, you are not the first person to do whatever it is that you do. I was not the first social media manager out there, so I had to work out what it was that made me different to others.

Now you need to break down the types of content that you share with your ecosystem. Yes, the same content can be shared across platforms; it just has to be repurposed in a way that works for the platform it is being shared on. When I really started getting intentional with the content I was sharing, that is when things start to move for me.

So, have a look at the content you are sharing:

Are you elevating yourself and telling people how awesome you are?

Are you sharing value that shows you know what you are talking about?

Are you polarising enough and really pushing away those you don't want to work with?

Are you inspiring people to take action?

And the most important one for anyone in business:

Have you told anyone what your service is recently?

Honestly, the amount of people I see that have not spoken about their offer in a while blows my mind. If you are not selling in your business, you have an expensive hobby.

I know that creating this content, really standing up and getting out of your own way can be scary. It takes a certain amount of confidence to be polarising and say, I don't want to work with you.

But nothing good ever comes from inside of your comfort zone.

Has my journey to this point been easy? Absolutely not, but it has helped me create a system that works, is scalable and will help other entrepreneurs to skip the corners, road bumps and the empty bank accounts that I encountered along the way, and ultimately grow their business without the hustle and the overheads. I am always learning, as social media develops and as business moves on, I am always looking at new ways that I can show my clients how they can step out of their comfort zone and do things a little differently.

Crafting an ecosystem is time-consuming. It is not a get-rich-quick scheme, but if you are in business for the long haul, then it is a fantastic way to attract clients in a way that is aligned, not sleazy or salesly, and it will make your business and sales seem so much easier than it ever has before.

One of my 1:1 clients came to me after trying to build a business for 2 years. She went back to work after not being able to craft her offer in a way that felt right for her and aligned with what she wanted to help her clients with. After a few sessions, we had mastered her uniqueness and crafted an offer that she was excited to sell. Soon after she had already told her boss and was ready to go all in on her business. She was ready to commit to the business and trusted that with the tools she now had she would 100% be able to make this work.

Another of my clients came to me and joined my 5 week Attract Dream Clients program. She was earning just £400 a month and within 5 weeks, scaled that up to £3000 per month, just with the skills she learnt along the way. The program gives you the tools to get visible using other people's Facebook groups. She understood that she needed to get more visible and to really showcase her skills in a different way to attract clients. Within the program she was able to do exactly that and now has the skills to do this on repeat every single month.

A client came to me recently with a large Facebook group but a lack of clients. We looked at the content and strategy she was using inside her Facebook group and within the first week, she had gone on to sign two of those group members just by changing the way she was communicating with them both inside the group and in conversations she was already having.

I promise you that business can be fun. There will be times you want to throw your head against a brick wall, times you will want to pop open the champagne and times you will want to smash your laptop. This could even happen all in the same day. But creating a life that you choose is worth getting outside of your comfort zone for.

Stop looking around for the answers and the shiny objects or the next funnel and start creating your ecosystem in a way that is sustainable and scalable.

Wherever you are in business, if you want to build a sustainable and scalable business then join the community here: www.deashawaddup.com/community or check out my podcast, Scaling With Deasha, available on all the places you would normally listen to podcasts.

ABOUT THE AUTHOR

Deasha Waddup is a Social Media and Business Coach who helps online service-based entrepreneurs to scale their business, using organic social media strategies.

Before starting to coach, Deasha built a social media management agency that helped 6 & 7 figure entrepreneurs with their organic social media and group growth. Deasha started coaching at the request of her clients and also wanted to help people that didn't yet have the large teams ready to hit the ground running with their social media presence. The social media management agency is still going and still helps clients with community management and social selling on Facebook.

Deasha enjoys running and will usually give any sport a go at least once.

Deasha is available for 1:1 coaching, group coaching and social media management.

You can reach Deasha at:

Email: deasha@deashawaddup.com

Website: www.deashawaddup.com

 facebook.com/socialtreats

 instagram.com/socialtreats

HELEN JANE

PERMISSION TO THROW AWAY THE RULE
BOOK.

For the first time in my life, I have given
myself permission to be me. Finally, I
have let go of most of the unwritten rules which kept
me shackled for so long: Rules that I had lived my life
by for as long as I can remember, often without realising. Rules passed down through the family generations.
Rules dictated by society.

I am now more confident than I have ever been as I
rediscover and connect with the real me. I am finally
allowing myself to let go of the decades of conditioning. I feel comfortable and confident making my own
decisions and choices, no longer influenced by others
or by society. As I step into my sixties, I recognise that
this is my time. Time for me to step up and to share my
wisdom. I recognise that life has happened for me and
not to me. I feel a sense of freedom and excitement.

Far from the perceived expectations of 'old age', I feel this is the 'new age for me'. A new decade with new opportunities. Possibilities without limitation because I have set myself free.

I am exactly where I am meant to be. After a few previous attempts and diversions, I am on the threshold of launching my business, bringing together much of my leaning and life experience which I feel compelled to share. It compiles my life's work so far. This is so precious to me. It has taken time, energy, and commitment to birth.

As soon as I stopped trying to be like everyone else, and following everyone else's blueprints, all the pieces began to slot into place. The struggle with life fell away as I stopped constantly pushing myself and began to feel the ebb and flow of energy that was within me - the cycles of energy and life that we all experience. Now, I am doing it my way, without the guilt and without the rule book.

I had lived my life according to the expectations of others, without realising it, for so long. I had a 'good' job with a well-known company. I thought I was happy, until it all began to fall apart. It was then I realised that I was living life on a hamster wheel. It was a safe life, with a pay packet at the end of each month, but such a struggle because I was living out of alignment. A battle physically and mentally. I experienced frequent periods of exhaustion and burnout.

Whilst in my thirties and forties, I had often thought of starting my own business. I craved the freedom to be me; to earn a living doing something that lit me up, that nourished my soul. Something always stopped me. I had been conditioned from an early age to play it safe. Business was risky. My father's business had failed when I was a small child. Later in life, my mother would share what a difficult time it had been for the family. A shameful time. It was much more sensible to play it safe, play it small, to play by the rules. That is exactly what I did.

There were times when I rebelled against this advice. As a girl, I loved animals and wanted to be a vet. I was told I was not clever enough. Besides, this was not a suitable job for a girl. Then I wanted to leave school at sixteen and go to college to become a makeup artist; I dreamt of travelling and working on film sets all over the world. This dream was quickly quashed too as I was told it was best to stay on at school to do my 'A' levels. I was frequently reminded how privileged I was to be a pupil at a girls' grammar school and to be getting a good education. I was a good student and did as I was told, although not always without a fight. At eighteen, I was urged to go to university. This time, I rebelled. I refused point blank. My parents and teachers were disappointed.

The excitement of travel was calling me. I went to work in International Banking. This was an 'acceptable job'. Steady and reliable, with the prospect of a good career and a final salary pension. I could not wait for my first overseas posting. The furthest I got was London on training courses. Not very international! After five years, I could stand it no longer and decided to leave after being offered a job in Italy working as a resort representative and tour guide. My family were horrified. How could I be so irresponsible? I remember my father saying to me *'You will never get a good job like this again! You are throwing your life away on some silly whim.'* Thank goodness, I thought. I felt stifled. I desperately wanted my father's approval, but it never came. I remember the look of disappointment as he waved me off at the station on the first leg of my journey to freedom. My mother was too upset to come to the station!

My time in Italy was the start of me getting to know me. I felt free, vibrant, alive. Life was exciting and fun. I loved my life and the opportunity to experience a new culture. We worked hard and partied even harder.

I remember one day, one of the head reps saying to me: *'Think carefully about your future. You don't want to end up like me. A middle-aged, single, lonely woman'.* Why would she say such a thing? Was she just jealous? I often heard her in my head. Her warning. I am sure this influenced my decision to return home a year later.

I quickly fell back into the generational pattern of safe and sensible. My family were delighted when I was offered a job at British Airways - another good job, another respectable company. I felt my life closing in. I was torn between pleasing my family and being me. The family won!

I remember my mother saying to me *'Now you will be able to settle down – you don't want to be left on the shelf.'* I was only 25!!!

I met my future husband shortly after. I had fallen back into following the rules.

The relationship was very on and off. In one of the off phases, I was offered a job working as a resort representative on Lake Garda. I was so excited; this was my dream job. When I shared the news with my family, it was greeted with dismay. My ex was soon back on the scene. I clearly remember the day I phoned the holiday company to turn the job down. I felt such inner turmoil, as though I was losing my freedom again. It was one of those defining moments in life. There have been a few of those.

I tried to convince myself that I was doing the right thing, but deep in my heart I knew it was the wrong decision. My soul yearned to travel but once again I was following the unwritten family rules.

I wonder if you can recognise yourself in this story. What are you not listening to? What calling are you ignoring? Whose rules are you following?

It was only when I allowed myself the time and space to stop and to listen that I started to hear my inner voice. It was only when I opened to opportunity and began to do the inner work that life began to change. When I started to put my needs first.

The on-off relationship continued. I was shown so many signs that this was not the relationship for me. Did I listen? No, I wanted to be in love. I was terrified of being left on the shelf. Perhaps I was looking for approval. I was desperate to fit in. Desperate to be loved. The fact was, I did not love or value myself.

Back then, I knew nothing of energy work, the law of vibration, the law of attraction and co-creating. Unwittingly, I had attracted my ideal man into my life, or so I thought. He was tall, dark, handsome, and foreign. After my time in Italy, I had no desire to settle down with one of those nice, boring English men. I had tasted the freedom and excitement of living overseas and I wanted to bring an element of that into my life in England. I look back now and can see how superficial this all was. I was looking externally to create my 'perfect' life. It was all an illusion.

The night before my fairy tale wedding, my father came into my bedroom and said to me '*You do not have to go through with this*'. I often wonder what he saw that I was blind to. I never did find out.

On the way to the church, we were stuck in traffic behind a steam roller, and we arrived thirty minutes late. Was this another sign I ignored? I now wonder. I laugh now when I share this story.

I was excited to be stepping into this new phase of my life. I now had almost everything I dreamed of. I was thrilled when my son, Andre, was born, twelve months later. It was love at first sight. I now had my 'perfect' little family. I thought that our first-born would bring my husband and I closer together. I wonder how many other women have thought the same thing. I was deluded. Things soon went from bad to worse.

Fast forward a few years, I should have been happy. Outwardly, I had all the trappings of success: a gorgeous son, a handsome husband, a lovely home, a nice car, and a good job.

The reality was that my husband expected me to follow his rules; to give up work and be a stay-at-home mum. By now, I had a position working at Manchester Airport. I loved the excitement of working at the airport. No two days were ever the same. I insisted on going back to work part-time and thought my husband would be supportive. He was not. I ended up burned out and contracted viral pneumonia. My son was nine months old at the time and we were in the middle of renovating a house. One night, I felt so ill I thought I was going to die. I remember lying on the bathroom floor, too weak to get up, thinking this is it, this is the end. I was seriously ill. The GP wanted to admit me to hospital, but my husband refused, saying I had a baby to look after!

My confidence and self-esteem were at an all-time low. I felt unloved and worthless. I was frightened to speak out; what was the point? No one would listen. No one would hear me.

Looking back, I had never felt good enough - not clever enough, not pretty enough.

I had watched generations of women playing small and settling for less. Only a couple of generations earlier, women had been defined by their marriage partners and this was still happening to me in the 1990s.

Still, I held on to the vague hope that it would all come good. That we would be that happy family I longed for.

We completed the house renovation and soon moved into our next home. It was a beautiful home, everything that I could possibly wish for. I remember saying to my ex-husband as we walked up the path of our new home '*If we can't be happy here, we will never be happy*'. How significant those words were to become? I loved my home but most of my time was spent alone. My ex-husband was working hard, but his spare time was spent with his friends, gambling. He would stay out until the early hours of the morning, often getting home just before I went to work at 5am.

In April 1993, my father passed away aged sixty-three. He had retired in the previous September and been diagnosed with terminal cancer the following January. He and my mother had dreams of travelling but in an instant, those dreams evaporated. I adored my father. He was a gentle man of few words, but had that air of inner strength. If only they had followed their dreams sooner. Losing him to such a brutal, unforgiving illness will haunt me forever. I decided on the day he died that I did not want to put my life on hold as he had.

A month after his death I was crying, as I thought, about my father. My ex-husband said to me '*You should be over that by now*'. How heartless!

That was the catalyst I needed, and I started thinking about leaving. It all happened very quickly after that.

Shortly after my ex-husband was going to visit his family overseas.

I remember saying to him *'When you come back, I won't be here.'*

His laughed as he responded *'You will never leave me. No-one else will ever want you!'*.

I cannot remember if I replied out loud or said the words in my head. My response was *'Just watch me!'*

His words wounded me like a knife. To this day I do not know where I found the strength and inner courage to leave. When he came back from his holiday, I had moved into my mother's house, sharing my child-hood bedroom with my three-year-old son.

It was not easy. I felt broken. My mother was fearful of what the neighbours would say!

My ex-husband begged me to go back. I was torn. Could I continue to endure the emotional abuse for the sake of our son? We had sold our joint home by then and both bought our own homes. I was in a state of real confusion and decided that I would give it another go. I called around to his house to tell him the good news only to find him with another woman. I was heartbroken. I had been drawn in by his lies again but this time, the universe was intervening.

There was no way back now.

In the following weeks and months, I fluctuated between feeling hopeless and excited.

The massive responsibility of being a single mother weighed heavily on me. There was so much stigma at the time. How would the breakup affect my son? Andre became my world; everything became about him. He was my reason to go on. I had to be strong for him.

In addition to looking after my son, I also took responsibility for my mother, who was grieving. She was not ready to be a widow. My feelings were pushed down. I had to be strong for everyone else.

I was consumed with guilt, the guilt of taking Andre away from his father, the guilt of working full time, the guilt of a failed marriage. Sometimes I would go out with friends, but the guilt was overbearing. I did not deserve to have fun; I did not deserve to put my needs first. That was selfish.

My mother would often remark on how strong I was. It was all an illusion. Inside I was falling apart. I was exhausted physically, mentally, and emotionally. I felt like a failure. Bouts of depression and stress followed, and my physical health suffered. My answer was always to carry on, to keep quiet. I did not dare ask for help, that was weak.

I was still desperate to be loved.

I had a couple of emotionally abusive relationships before meeting the 'love of my life' at Christmas in 2002. Life improved massively. We spent as much time together as possible and travelled often. We went on Caribbean cruises, flew on Concorde, and holidayed in Florida, Las Vegas, Boston, Sedona, South Africa, and Spain. We bought properties in Florida and Spain. We were having fun building memories and often talked about our future together. We started house hunting. Looking at beautiful properties in Derbyshire, halfway between his home and mine. I was so happy when on my birthday in 2005 'the love of my life' surprised me with the most beautiful Tiffany engagement ring. Surely my life was now complete and on track. The reality was that I now had someone else's needs to put before my own. Still, I thought this was my forever relationship and more than worth the effort. I was in love. We were blissfully happy. I had finally found someone who loved me, someone I could build a future with. When friends started to voice concerns about his controlling ways, I ignored them. They did not know him like I did. I convinced myself they were jealous. Then it all unravelled, rather quickly and dramatically. The 'love of my life' had been under a lot of stress with his business, or that is what he told me. He made excuses not to spend weekends with me because he was working. He sounded stressed, he was not answering my calls, he said he was unable to sleep. I was very worried. In May 2007, I spoke to a joint friend and expressed my concerns. He suggested I drive over to his house. It was another one of those moments when life stands still when I found 'the love of my life' with another woman. History was repeating itself. I took my beautiful engagement ring off and threw it at him (Fortunately, I had the foresight to pick it up again before I left)!

I was heartbroken again. Funny how the pattern was repeating itself.

I fell into a deep depression. Life did not seem worth living any more.

Even my son blamed me for the relationship breakdown.

I decided it was all my fault and began to go through the if onlys....

I was still unable to see this was about me and the universe was giving me signs to do the inner work.

Now it is so clear, I did not love and value myself. All my life I had invested my time and energy in others. I let myself be trampled over. I was the proverbial doormat. I had no self-respect, no confidence, and no self-esteem. I was a people pleaser. The only person I did not try to please was myself.

I felt broken. Life was so unfair, so cruel.

At this point I was unable to see the patterns and lessons I was being shown. Life was happening to me and I allowed it to happen. I did not know there was another way.

Surely, I had hit rock bottom? But, no. There was more to come.

A couple of weeks later we were served notice at work. The airline was closing the base at Manchester Airport and all the staff were facing redundancy or redeployment.

I could not believe how my life was playing out. I felt as if I were in quicksand, sinking deeper and deeper.

For the next few months, I felt as though I was living a nightmare. Due to ill health my mother was now living with me and my son. I was responsible for us all. I was grieving for my relationship and my job, but I had to remain strong for them. Those were the rules.

I made the decision to relocate to Heathrow and retrain as long-haul cabin crew. The airline business and travel industry were all I had known for more than twenty years; now in my mid-forties I did not believe I was able do anything else. Of course, this decision was made at an incredibly low point in my life. I was in survival mode and unable to see, let alone consider, any other alternatives.

Each time I set out on the five-hour drive to Heathrow, I felt sick. I cried myself to sleep, alone in hotel rooms. Other people would have given their right arm to have the opportunity I had been given, I told myself. I thought there was something wrong with me.

Then it struck me that I was, once again, doing what I had been told to do.

I did not have the courage, confidence, or self-esteem to consider other options.

I was still not listening to me, to my inner voice. I still had my head buried in the sand. I can still feel the emotions of leaving my family to go on another trip. Meeting a different crew for each trip. Spending my time with strangers instead of with my loved ones. I was deeply unhappy and very lonely.

In 2008; I came across the Law of Attraction and started to consider how I had manifested my life. Part of me thought it was a load of rubbish and part of me was intrigued. I started to toy with the idea of a new relationship and wrote down a list of some of the qualities I would like in a man. Wow, did the universe deliver. Within a couple of weeks, I had met my current partner. He fitted the criteria even down to the hair colour and height. Maybe there was something in this Law of Attraction theory after all. I put it down to coincidence, as many people do. Little did I realise the synchronicities happening in my life.

By now, I was half listening. I was curious and started to read lots of books. I then got to the point where I thought that the Law of Attraction theory worked for others but not for me. Meeting my partner had been a fluke.

My partner knew I hated the job and told me to leave. I would often ring him in tears from Heathrow, before I boarded my flight. He would say '*Just come home. Think of what you are doing to yourself*'.

How could I? I had my son and my mother to consider. They were my priority, not me.

The thought of relying on anyone else terrified me. I had learned to be self-sufficient. It was dangerous to rely on others. No one else was to be trusted, especially not men. I recognise this now as a reflection of my lack of self-worth.

I had to carry on. My son was due to go to university in the October.

Once again, I was not listening and then, as often happens, I was forced to listen.

In October 2008 I was on a flight from San Francisco to Heathrow when the 747 I was on suffered a heavy landing. I was sitting over the undercarriage and felt the wheels bounce off the runway and then hit it again. Overhead lockers flew open as the aircraft shook violently. Fellow cabin crew stated that it was the heaviest landing they had experienced in over twenty years.

Over the course of the next couple of days I began to suffer with neck and back pain and went off sick. The pain increased over the following few weeks, and my mobility was being affected. By the time I was referred for physiotherapy, I was bent over, unable to stand up straight. The pain was excruciating. For weeks, the physiotherapy continued. I felt as if no one was listening when I told them how much pain I was in. That familiar story! Eventually I was sent for an MRI scan. The scan revealed slipped disks in my neck and lower back. The only option I was told was surgery.

And here is the interesting part. My partner worked at the time for the NHS in the operating theatres. Somehow, he was able to bump me up the list and get the best team together for the surgery. I was so grateful. For once I was in the right place at the right time. Shame the circumstances were not more pleasing.

I assumed after the surgery I would be able to get back to work.

How wrong I was.

Months after the surgery, I was still in considerable pain and taking heavy medication. It was at this point that I was made to listen when the surgeon told me that if I went back to my job, I would suffer with severe chronic pain. It was another of those moments when time stood still.

I had no choice. I left my job. I was forced to sell my home, spend Andre's university fund, and move in with my partner. My mother moved back into her own home, which had been rented out, and my son moved in with his father.

I felt as if my life was falling apart. In fact, it was the old parts of my life falling away to rebuild something new, something for me. For the first time in my life, unable to work, I was given the space and time to consider what I wanted. At my lowest, I thought about taking my own life because I was so frightened, staring into this empty void. I was in my late forties. I felt like my life was over. Then, slowly, I began to see that I had been living my life for everyone else, as so many women do. This was to become the start of my reawakening. The time that I began to listen.

There were still a few more pieces of the jigsaw which needed to fall into place before I was ready to start to rebuild my life.

I began to think about what brought me real fulfil-ment. I had always loved helping others and I was able to see the potential they chose not to see. This encouraged me to become accredited as a life coach and to take a qualification in teaching. I managed to find employment working with people who were unemployed, suffering with low confidence and self-esteem, then I was made redundant twice due to funding ending. My next role was working for a mental health charity, supporting people with depression, anxiety, stress, and low confidence, before being made redundant again and transferred into a role I did not enjoy.

I can see now that the universe was constantly nudging me. Encouraging me to follow my dreams, to follow my purpose.

The universe still had a few more nasty surprises for me to deal with, a few more chains to break, before I finally felt free to build my life. To finally put myself first.

My mother suffered a stroke in 2012 and came to live with my partner and I shortly after. Sadly, she was diagnosed with vascular dementia and passed away in 2015. This was a real blow to me. I had stepped into a role caring for my mother and this left a huge void in my life. She spent the last few months of her life in a care home. The guilt of putting her into care still haunts me.

Then my son and his partner decided to move to New Zealand, emigrating in 2017. I felt bereft. The only thing I had left to look after now was my cat. He crossed the rainbow bridge in 2018 aged 18.

There was nothing left to look after.

I was staring into a black empty void.

The final push was being the victim of workplace bullying at the mental health charity. It was then I made the decision to leave and set up my own business.

I was in my mid-fifties when I summoned the courage to focus on me. I enrolled on every course I came across that promised the elusive change I was looking for. Eventually, I realised that it was not about learning something new, it was about reconnecting and rediscovering me: developing the skills and knowledge I already had within; following my heart and doing the things that lit me up from inside, not the promise of money from learning someone else's blueprint or method.

Can you see the pattern again?

Listening to someone else and not to myself, ignoring my inner voice, my intuition?

This time, it was about going deep within and finding those things that resonated with me. And that is exactly what I did. I took the time and energy to discover, or rather rediscover, me. I say rediscover because I believe that we all know innately what serves us, if only we allow ourselves the time and space.

We are our most precious piece of work, our greatest investment. It isn't selfish or arrogant, but absolute necessity to put our needs first.

Over the years, I have worked with hundreds of people with low confidence and self- esteem, stress, anxiety, and depression. The majority were women just like me. Women who had spent all their lives looking after others and were now left, at midlife, with that empty void in front of them and wondering how to fill it.

I gently supported these women to reconnect with themselves and encouraged them to start dreaming again. To put themselves first and to take baby steps to create a life that is fulfilling. Helping them to let go of the guilt and the confusion as they approached the next important phase of their life. Helping them to develop hope and optimism.

Many of these women said that they felt they had lost their purpose. I now believe we can have many purposes, depending on the stage of our life. I helped them to reconnect with and reawaken the purpose they had put on hold.

Some have gone on to build new careers, some have set up their own businesses, others have started new relationships. The one thing they have in common is that they are now living life on their terms, with intention.

It saddens me that so many women still go through such difficult times during their forties and beyond - surviving divorce, teenagers, children leaving home, redundancy, bereavement, ageing parents, menopause, health problems... and end up feeling lost and invisible.

This is no longer about someone telling you what the rules to your life are. It is about writing your own rules. Your rules. Rules that serve you and which will create a life you love. It is about giving yourself the opportunity to get to know yourself again. To spend time nurturing yourself, your soul, your whole being, as you awaken from your long slumber.

I knew that there must be more to life. I became curious and started to be open to opportunity. At first, I tried to figure all this out on my own, independent and taking responsibility for myself. My rule book told me not to ask for help as it showed weakness. To show vulnerability would mean putting myself at risk and being seen as weak.

There is a saying, 'When the student is ready, the teacher will appear'. This is so true of my journey. As I became more curious, books and courses were suggested to me. I had a real thirst for knowledge.

Eventually I allowed others to support and guide me. It was not easy to allow others in, but this was a real turning point in my life. I have been so fortunate to be guided by some wonderful teachers. The difference was, this time they were not telling me what to do; they were guiding me to discover what worked for me. Call it what you will; intuition, higher self, inner guidance, inner knowing, gut feeling. Instinctively we know what is right and wrong for us, if we allow ourselves that time and space.

For years I had worked on my mindset, but now I was delving into energy work and working on the conscious and unconscious mind. To me, the key is to work on energy, mindset, and the conscious and subconscious mind simultaneously. A more holistic approach which creates flow.

I have used a variety of methodologies to change my life, which I will highlight here. I know these work because they work for me. I know they will work for you too.

- Coaching tools to help identify where you are and what you would like to change. The wheel of life is a helpful tool to start with. If you don't know where you are, how will you know what you want to change and how will you measure the changes that take place?

- The Energy Alignment Method ™ (EAM), a methodology created by Yvette Taylor. This method helps you to tune into your own energy to discover what is holding you back. You may think it is one thing but often, when you tune into your energy, you discover it is not what you thought. Using EAM can quickly identify the blocks without having to relive the pain and discomfort of past events. You can also release generational patterns, freeing generations to come. It is an amazing life changing tool!

- Energy Editing ™, created by Michelle Lowbridge, which again is a simple tool to work on your energy to release beliefs, emotions and patterns that no longer serve you.

- Hypnotherapy to reprogramme your subconscious and create positive change. Hypnotherapy is an amazing tool to help with anxiety, stress, weight loss, phobias, PTSD, trauma, menopausal symptoms, and pain management.

- I also work on yin and yang energy, the masculine and the feminine, using nature and the lunar cycles. Are you supporting your feminine energy or are you still in the push of masculine energy? Spending too long in that

masculine push, action-taking energy will
without doubt lead to burnout.

- As I began to do the work on myself, I felt as
  if I were weighed down with clutter. Mental,
  energetic, emotional, and physical clutter. I
  now incorporate elements of space clearing
  and Feng Shui into my work. The benefits
  from clearing your space and energy are
  incredible.

I have worked with hundreds of people, mainly midlife
women, and witnessed them change their lives when
they start to do the inner work, letting go of the
limiting beliefs and patterns and changing their energy.
This is so much more than repeating affirmations and
journaling - I see that as the supportive work, but the
deeper work is what creates the lasting transformation.

Clients have changed their lives completely once they
have put themselves first. Their physical and mental
health has improved; they have let go of relationships
that no longer serve them and stepped into lives that
bring them joy and abundance. This is not about fixing
someone, it is about helping them reawaken their inner
dreams, reconnecting with their soul and their purpose
which has always been within them.

Instead of racing through life, I now enjoy each deli-
cious phase. Recently, I have become interested in the

Chinese 5 elements. Life is full of cycles. I never saw this before. I am becoming more and more aware of the cycles of life. We are surrounded by cycles - we only need to observe nature. I am incorporating more and more of this into my life and into my work. As human beings, we are taught to fight against these cycles, not to listen to our bodies. Is it any wonder that there is so much stress in the world? We are taught to push through; to keep going when are bodies are screaming 'Stop!'. When we do not listen, there can be dramatic and often life-changing consequences.

As women, as we reach our forties, fifties, and sixties, we are stepping into the most important and influential stages of our lives.

Western society may insinuate that we are past it, that we have had the best years of our lives. We can allow society to define our roles and purpose, or we can define our own. For a moment, consider the wealth of knowledge and experience you have to share. As young women, we may feel that we have a wonderful life ahead of us but then somehow, we allow others to hijack our dreams. The pressure can be intense as the biological clock ticks by. Before we know it, we are stepping into what can be the most glorious years. The years when we can truly be ourselves. When we stop caring what others think, when our beauty does come from within. You can either stay lurking in the shadows, thinking '*Is this it?*', or you can take the decision to make these years matter. That is my purpose; to help older women recognise their wisdom and innate power. To encourage them to step out and to serve their communities in a different way. To recognise that their life has mattered and continues to matter.

There is more to life and more to you. It is waiting to be reawakened.

I hope by taking the time to read my chapter you are beginning to consider the potential within you. Recognising that your purpose is not something you have to seek, but something that already resides within. And yes, we may have many different purposes at different stages of life.

Are you beginning to appreciate the gifts in your life experience?

Everything is already there for you to begin to reconnect with your purpose. Is it time for you to write a new rule book as you reawaken from your slumber? Notice the subtle signs. The feelings of resistance, the voice that keeps whispering to you. It is time for you to start listening to you.

I urge you not to choose the path I did for so long; living my life by someone else's rules. It does not have to be so hard. Uncomfortable, yes, because change can be uncomfortable. Stepping out of our comfort zone into the unknown can be scary. I am now on a mission to guide women to discover the magic that comes in the latter part of life as they throw away the rule book, awaken from their slumber and develop the courage to follow long held dreams. If my mission calls to you and you would like support, I would love to share my seven step P.U.R.P.O.S.E Programme with you. This has evolved from my own life experience and is designed to support you on your journey.

In closing, I wish you a life of fulfilment and joy as you reawaken your purpose and throw away the rule book.

ABOUT THE AUTHOR

HELEN JANE

Helen is an international best-selling author and award-winning influencer, creator of Reawaken your Purpose and the P.U.R.P.O.S.E Programme.

Helen uses many methodologies with her clients. She is one of the first 16 certified Energy Alignment Method Mentors, a Certified Life Coach, a qualified Clinical Hypnotherapist, registered with the GHR, and an Akashic Record Consultant, certified by The Souls Journeys Method.

After more than 25 years of working in the travel industry, at the age of 48, Helen suffered a serious back injury and was forced to resign from her job without knowing what she would do next. Her life began to unravel as she lost her home, her relationship, dealt with bereavement and her only son emigrating to New Zealand.

Suffering from depression and burnout Helen felt lost, unseen, unheard and without hope as she stepped into her 50's.

Over the course of the last 10 years, Helen has not only turned her own life around but in her roles as a coach, mental health practitioner and mentor, she has worked with hundreds of people, the majority of them women, supporting them to do the same. She has written and delivered numerous courses to help others to reduce stress and anxiety, to build confidence and self-esteem and to live a more purposeful life. She has also run online trainings and retreats for women.

Helen is passionate in her work of guiding women to set themselves free from generational patterns and the expectations of others and society, to rediscover them- selves. Helping them to discover the magic that comes in the important second half of their lives, as they step out of the shadows, reignite their passion for life and develop the confidence and courage to rediscover a new purpose and to follow their dreams

Contact details:

email hello@helencjane.co.uk

website: https://www.helencjane.co.uk/

 facebook.com/helencjane
instagram.com/helencjane
linkedin.com/in/helencjane

JO GILBERT

PERMISSION TO LIVE LIFE YOUR WAY

" "Jo you are so lucky"

— MOST PEOPLE

For many years now, friends, family, colleagues and strangers have described me, I guess without too much thought, as 'lucky'.

I hear expressions like '*OMG Jo you're so lucky to have such a beautiful house*' or '*You're so lucky to own that car*' or '*Jo you're so lucky you go on all of those holidays*' or '*You're lucky because you've got a good job*' and more recently '*You're so lucky to live in Lanzarote*'.

In fact insert whatever it is that is going on in my life at a particular time which is remotely positive and 'I'm lucky' is the standard perception.

Really? Does this happen to you, can you relate?

For example, I regularly share my daily exercise routine via my instagram story, so my accountability partners can see I am indeed doing what I said I would do towards my health goals. I'm not entirely sure when the alarm clock goes off when I've only been in bed for a few hours just how lucky I am or feel. I work late in to the night and I get up so early every morning to walk 8.5km to stay in shape and healthy before I sit down in my office at 8:30am to start what is usually another 14 or 16-hour working day, again I don't think thats lucky either, more on that later.

In all honesty I would much prefer to stay in bed! So the fact that I don't, is that luck or is that motivation, determination and self discipline? Perhaps people perceive it to be lucky because it's a 8.5kms walk along the coastal path and lava fields of Playa Blanca, Lanzarote, the most exceptionally stunning scenery for an early morning walk. However, the very fact that its still dark some mornings when I set off and if I don't do it I would probably only get 300 steps in a day is seemingly irrelevant.

I have so many other examples of my perceived luck, so I felt I needed to address this perception of how lucky I am and share my story of overcoming some extreme adverse events and situations. I wrote my first book 'Strength & Power' which became a #1 Amazon Best seller in May 2018 and held the top spot in several categories for a couple of weeks, how 'lucky' insert rolling eyes emoji!

I'd love for you to read my back story, to get an insight into my journey to becoming a successful business entrepreneur and living life on my terms (with the exception of how early I have to get up to exercise). In my book, I share some of the tools and techniques I use every day to keep me moving forwards by taking focused, purposeful and positive action to achieve my goals.

For the record, luck to me is walking down the street and picking a fiver up off the pavement, or perhaps having a cheeky win on the lotto or scratch card. Its also that amazing moment when the server leaves the brandy bottle on your table for you to help yourself for after dinner drinks, happy days!

LET ME SHARE WITH YOU MY SLIDING DOORS MOMENT

It was November 2017, I was 46 years old, life had taken a few very unexpected twists and turns in recent months and I found myself at a crossroads in life.

As I lay in my hospital bed, with sepsis for the second time in 10 years, I couldn't help but think of all the things I wish I had done or wanted to do, but never did because I always put myself last. It didn't matter who you were, friend, family member or acquaintance if you needed my time, my money, my support, I would sacrifice my wishes, dreams and desires to fulfil yours.

Some may see that as quite noble and caring thing to do, but let me tell you, when you think you are about to kick the bucket and you look around you at your bedside to see who has taken time out of their day to visit you or send you a message of support it can be quite a sobering moment - none of those people were anywhere to be found.

All of those time, money and mood hoovers were no where to be seen. Much to my absolute joy, my best friend Abigail Horne was there moonwalking around my bed, singing, making me laugh and encouraging me to get well. My only regret as I made the decision to live life on my terms that week was it would mean putting over 2500 miles in distance between us. The same sadness and regret was felt for my family to, who I also left behind. Although I don't think anyone believed me when I said I was leaving the UK soon.

Authors & Co was being bought to life at the time by Abigail and so shortly after leaving the hospital in full support of her new company I started to write my book. As I recalled my life events and achievements, I could see it was time for me to be put first for a change. Queue the adventure! In January of 2018, myself and Abigail went on one hell of a girls holiday to Singapore and then onto five days in Bali on an Ultimate Human Experience retreat. We came back from that holiday changed women ready to take on our next chapters in this short journey we call life.

At the end of March, with my book almost written and ready to publish, I had another near death experience after my rescue dog dragged me through a snowy, icy woodland path, he airborne threw me into a tree and concrete steps and I landed within inches of a spike sticking up from the ground next to my chest. Without a doubt it would've killed me if I had landed on it, instead I escaped with two broken hands and a tear to my right bicep.

Three days later I was heading to Lanzarote with both hands in splints and my right arm in a sling, flying solo and having to ask anyone who was willing to help to lift and carry my luggage for me. You see thats the type of person I am, despite the set back I was not going to cancel my plans so I went ahead with my holiday.

My book is all about over coming adversity and making it meaningful. There would be nothing over-come or meaningful in cancelling my plans and letting my friend down who was expecting me to villa and dog sit, that would have been an admission of defeat in my eyes. I always find a way to press ahead and yes sometimes it is a challenge, but its always worth it and fulfilling.

I had seen an episode of A Place in the Sun a few days before I arrived in Lanzarote and I was telling a family friend whilst out for a curry, that I had seen him on the show and one of the villas he had shown the family around is the kind of villa I would love to live in 'one day'. That villa was still up for sale and he could show it to me the next day! I just said yes ok lets do it. I had no idea how at that moment in time I could possibly move to Lanzarote as my work and home was all in the UK. My savings were tied up in properties I owned. I would have to sell them first before I could move and also think about how I would earn money on an island, in a country that speaks Spanish and I don't.

The villa was beautiful, but who was I kidding it was just a pipe dream really as my husband would have to give up his job as a motorbike instructor to move and I didn't think this would ever happen. He had just turned 50, so the prospect of leaving what he knew behind at this stage in his life would be a huge ask. Not to mention I would need to sell three properties to release capital to buy our place in the sun. The stars would definitely need to align to make this even remotely possible.

When I got back home to the UK, I showed Craig the photos and videos of the villa and I think he could see in my eyes, my presence and mood, just everything about me was longing for just once in my life to grab it by the balls and say *'fuck it lets go, I'm choosing to put myself first!'*

To my absolute surprise Craig looked at me and said, *"Lets do it, fuck it, you've been so ill and nearly died, let's just do it now before anything else happens to you"*. I didn't wait for him to change his mind! How many times did I have to become so ill that I would re-evaluate my life before I would just do it?

I carefully considered, what is the worst that can happen? We don't like it and come back? We might lose some money? That wasn't a big enough reason this time to stop me from going.

I put my houses up for sale, all of them sold within a few days. We sold large household items or gave things away, and I also hired a 5 tonne skip and went through the single most cathartic exercise ever, downsizing my life and belongings, I went from a three bedroom detached house with double garage and loft space full of 'stuff' to, if it didn't fit in one of four big red suitcases we weren't taking it with us. My god we don't half accumulate some crap over the years, like old birthday cards saved - why? Who looks at them? Old curtains, I had taken down to replace with new ones, why were they in storage filling a wardrobe shelf, I was never going to put them up again. Why do we do that? It can't be just me.

From a pipe dream whilst on holiday in early April to boarding a flight on 17th June 2018, alone with three of the suitcases, leaving my husband and two rescue dogs behind, I set off for my new life in the sunshine.

Craig and the dogs would follow me two weeks later once the dogs flight was due and the house sale had completed.

Becoming an expat has been three things for me;

1. **Heart wrenching**. I terribly miss being able to nip to see my daughter and grandson Finley, and my sister Jenny. I miss Friday afternoon pub lunches with Abigail and being able to have impromptu nights out or work days together. FaceTime has become my lifeline.
2. **Life Changing**. Health wise, I get to exercise everyday, I get a daily top up of Vitamin D. My diet has completely changed, I was a daily junk food consumer of Justeat to now eating healthy most days and only having a meal out once or twice a week, and even then the food is so much healthier. I get to visit the beach

and sit by the ocean whenever I want to, just so many things. I also have the best laughs with Shaz, I could write another solo book on this amazing woman, she is an absolute tower of strength and one of the most incredibly selfless, loving and caring, funny, beautiful women I have ever had the privilege to call my friend.

3. **Business and Career Booming**. I don't know if it's the sea air, the sunshine, the change of lifestyle or a combination of all these things, however I have never felt so motivated to do more and achieve more. I haven't been into the office where I used to work in the Uk since July 2020 so almost a year now. I had been commuting back to the Uk frequently prior to covid-19 spending 2-3 days per week in the Uk office and long weekends at home, my carbon foot print from flights and motorway travel was horrendous. In my full-time corporate role, I am the Chief Operating Officer of a fully licensed gas and electricity supplier in the Uk. Although I'm now home-based showing up for all my meetings with clients and colleagues via MS Teams from my office in Lanzarote. I also work freelance with my best friend in her

publishing company for 3.5 years (the interior creation and design of this book is my work and quite possibly my last collaboration book to work on too, as I hang up my formatting boots to focus on new projects). Since moving to Lanzarote, I have also found time to be a part-time business coach and support lots of other businesses from a variety of sectors, supporting them to improve their operating models, cashflow and growth. I'm not one to sit on my hands, so, I am also about to launch my new consumer champion service CUBES. Right now I spend more time on my businesses and corporate career than I ever have, the difference is though that I work on my terms. If I want to go for a walk I do. If I want to work from a cafe or beach front I do. If I want to jump in the spa and relax I do. If I want to work the weekend and take a few early finishes during the week I do. Life is on my terms, my way. No commute has given me so much time back to live.

So, thats what happened when I decided to choose what I wanted in life and put my dreams and desires ahead of everyone else's. I don't sweat the smaller stuff anymore, I guess saying yes to 'me' in such a big life changing way has made the trivial, smaller choices easier. For the record my pasty pale skin tone is now looking a much healthier golden brown, I no longer look like I've just escaped from the morgue.

Now, I'm not suggesting for one minute that you should pack up your life and become an expat, far from it, it's not for everyone, however if thats a dream of yours my advice would be to just do it, bite the bullet and make it happen. You only live one short life here on this earth, even if you live to 100 years thats still a minuscule amount of time compared to an eternity dead (as none of us can say with any certainty what happens next, its all faith based not fact based). Life is too short to wait and not promised to anyone, tomorrow may be too late.

On a much smaller scale you can choose to say 'yes' to yourself more often and also 'no' to others and what doesn't serve you.

For example, '*Do you want to come to my child's 7th Birthday party?*' - standard answer now is '*no thank you but have a lovely afternoon*' where previously I would've said '*oh how lovely of course when is it?*' or a favourite of mine is '*Are you free on Saturday?*' now, before answering these leading questions with a '*yes why?*' I now say '*I'm not sure what my plans are without checking my diary?*' Why do I do that? Well, we all know leading questions are usually followed by a task question like '*will you....*' or '*could you....*' '*do you mind...*'. By saying I'm not sure of my plans I need to check, I've already given myself the perfect introduction to saying '*no thanks*' and doing something I want to do instead.

A quick exercise for you to think about with a cuppa

Grab yourself a cuppa, a brew, coffee. Get some paper or a journal and write these two lists out:

- What things in your life would you like to say 'yes' to or do more of?
- What things in your life would you like to say 'no' to or do less of?

You have to be really honest here, don't let thoughts of how your choices will impact others get in the way of you writing down your true desires. My grandson was only 17-months old when I boarded that plane in June 2018.

Finley is my little super hero, we spend so much quality time together since I left the Uk. We video call everyday sometimes two or three times a day. We still play together, role play the Avengers most days, eat, drink, laugh, cry, watch TV, youtube, read all the things.

When I fly to the Uk to visit or to fetch him its for quality time. Whereas if I was in the Uk permanently it would be a visit for an hour or two each week. He now comes to Lanzarote for a couple weeks or even months at a time. I actually see him more now than when I lived in the Uk. It's the same with my daughter Beckii and my friendship with Abi, it is as strong as ever. Distance is an obstacle to overcome thats all, you just have to work at these things and adapt.

Things I now say YES to easily

- Shall we go out for tea?
- Shall we buy this new TV?
- Do you fancy a change of Sofa?
- Shall I buy that car?
- Do you fancy going to the beach?
- Shall we book a Cruise?
- Shall we take the day off?
- Do you fancy changing the decor in here?
- Shall we buy that painting?
- Do you fancy a bottle of champagne?
- Do you fancy a takeout for tea?
- Do you want to go walk up that mountain?
- Shall we invite 'insert family member name here' to come stay with us for a holiday?
- Shall we get a new rescue dog?
- Do you fancy going for a coffee?

- Do you fancy sitting and watching the ferry come in and out?

Hopefully you get the idea?

<u>Things I now say NO to</u>

- Can you come into the office 5 days a week?
- Can you be in the Uk a couple of weeks each month?
- Do you want to come over for my child's party? (no thank you I'm 50 and my tolerance levels for screaming kids is limited to my grandson only).
- Are you cleaning up? (I'll do it when I'm ready not when I'm asked, our homes will always need cleaning and tidying, the sun may not always be shining)
- Can you do this for me 'insert thing'?
- Can you borrow me 'insert amount' I'll pay you back?

The 'no' list is shorter but again you get the general idea. There is so much I say 'no' to now, I will listen, but I don't rush in to save and prop up any more.

When I decided to live life my way, everything changed for the better. Don't get me wrong I've still had some tough times since we've moved here it's not all been sunshine and sangria. It's a completely different way of life, but without sounding too cheesy, if I can do it then you can do it too.

I love this quote;

> You are a product of your environment. So choose an environment that will best develop you towards your goals.

— AUTHOR UNKNOWN

HEATING OR EATING

If you do happen to read my solo book you will discover my background and lived experience of a rise from domestic abuse, benefits and poverty to the successes in business and the career I enjoy today.

I have worked in the Uk energy industry for twenty-two years now. Starting at entry level administrator right the way up to Chief Operating Officer for several companies and also Founder of my own passion project and consumer champion company CUBES.

Because of where I've come from, my grass roots so to speak, I have such a passion for alleviating fuel poverty and ensuring no one should ever have to choose between heating their home or eating a decent meal especially in the year 2021! My next book shares it's name with this section of my chapter and it really is relevant to 'living life your way'.

I now live my personal life my way. However for many years I have held my tongue on how the energy industry is run, and constantly fails consumers. So I haven't been living my 'professional life my way!' I have stayed silent and conformed, I have gone along with the insanity to ensure the money rolled in every month.

Twenty-two years of the same things over and over again. Customers phone in to contact centres and email customer service desks day in day out with the same queries and complaints in massive volumes every day, I'm talking thousands of you every single day. The exact same issues for twenty-two years!! It's like groundhog day!

Why? Because no one has ever challenged the norm. No one has ever empowered the consumer to do anything other than complain.

> "The definition of insanity is doing the same thing over and over again and expecting a different result".
>
> — ALBERT EINSTIEN

Is that the best service and solution I can provide for consumers, my friends, my family? What about my colleagues who have to listen to frustrated and angry customers day in day out. Is that really customer service and a great experience?

Did you even know that millions of households are having to make the sad and difficult choice of either heating their homes or putting food on the table. This is not just about customer service and complaints, this is also about affordability and getting treated fairly, getting a fairly priced tariff and not being ripped off. The industry is so complicated more than half the Uk households don't even engage with it so get stuck on really crap and expensive tariffs.

Companies set up to help consumers switch known as Price Comparison Websites are bumping up the price of energy tariffs with expensive commission rates and yet peddling the message to their users that the service is free! No, it is not free, it is convenient yes, but free, no!

Martin Lewis - Money Savings Expert appears on the Sunday Times Rich List with a Net Worth of £123m, impressive! (He didn't accrue that size of wealth from offering 'free' energy savings advice clearly!).

YOU the consumer always pay. Commission is built into your prices read the small print, suppliers have to pay them, you have to pay the supplier.

It's the same with door to door sales and telesales, you are paying for the sale. I will expand on this more in CUBES community.

OFGEM the energy regulator and organisations like Citizens Advice try to help but their measures are to treat the effects of a broken industry — stick a plaster on it, give it a pill, give them some compensation, say sorry. It's the same for the energy ombudsman, if you've got that far the industry has sadly already failed you.

No-one is saying let's try to approach this differently. With absolute certainty, I can tell you what the forecast for complaints and customer satisfaction will be for the next ten years if we keep doing the same thing, we will get more of the same.

I can't sit on my hands, tight lipped any longer, I can't stay quiet anymore. I need to speak out and '**live my professional life on my terms too!'**.

It's coming, I have found my voice and I actually feel more passionate about saying YES to this decision than I do about moving to Lanzarote. This decision is going to impact millions of lives in a positive way.

My life needed aligning in all areas not just my personal life. You the reader, you are my mission, we are all consumers, we all deserve great service. We all deserve to live and work our lives our way!

Customer Utility Bills Expertly Serviced is launching this autumn. It is not free, I do have a brand new service to sell, the pricing will be transparent and worth every penny, I wont be hiding charges because that is not ethical and honest. You will know exactly what you are paying us and what service you are getting in return, I guarantee it will be the lowest price service anyone can offer.

It can also be free, genuinely, you can do this yourself for free, in the CUBES Community I will show you how.

We all deserve better service and to heat and power our homes with food on the table that should never be a choice.

Things need to change, and someone needs to bring about that change! So, why not me, why not now, if I don't try we will never know and those groundhog days will remain forever.

I look forward to serving you in the autumn and ensuring as we go in to winter 2021, you are better equipped to keep the lights on and food on the table.

I make a promise to you right now;

> " I see you. I hear you. I am you. I've got you!

— JO GILBERT - FOUNDER CUBES

ABOUT THE AUTHOR
JO GILBERT

Jo has worked in the UK gas and electricity industry for the past 22 years. She is an entrepreneur, multiple business owner and investor.

In May 2018 Jo became an international #1 Amazon Best Selling Author with her first book on overcoming adversity, 'Strength & Power', later that year securing her second #1 Amazon Best Seller with the collaboration book 'She Who Dares'.

Jo has launched and supported several UK energy companies to market in her role as an Industry Expert, Business Strategist and Consultant.

Jo is the Founder of Utility Cubes Ltd, known simply as CUBES (Customer Utility Bills Expertly Serviced). This brand new consumer champion service will be launching in the Autumn of 2021 for UK households. To register your interest you can contact hello@utilitycubes.co.uk.

You can contact Jo:

Email: jo@utilitycubes.co.uk

Website: www.utilitycubes.co.uk

Or socially connect with Jo:

facebook.com/jo.gilbert.313

instagram.com/jo_gilbert3

linkedin.com/in/joannemgilbert

PERMISSION TO REST AND RECEIVE

 *erris Bueller said it well:*

> *"Life moves pretty fast. If you don't stop and look around once in a while, you could miss it".*

This is one of my favourite movies. And the cheeky high school student is right, sometimes we need to skip class occasionally to go on adventure. When was that last time you took a day off from work? I mean really a day off. One that is 100% dedicated to you. One where you unplugged 100%. One where you did not 'quickly check your messages in case something popped up?' One where you are fully present, being open for adventure and flow, seeing what the day brings, enjoying life to the fullest, doing what energises you and living your best life? A day without having to worry about work, your business and everything that is going on? Living in true time wealth?

Business is a fickle beast and most business owners tend to accept the fate of being dragged into a never-ending spiral of hard work, dedication and lack of free time in pursuit of the dream. What if this didn't need to be your reality? What if there was another way?

This chapter is designed to get you thinking outside of the box, help you diagnose the issues that plague your business, interrupt your productivity, and create a strategy to remove some of the roadblocks that are in between you and your goals. I have been there myself. I have slaved away, doing 80-hour weeks. I have forfeited my income because I felt my business couldn't afford to pay me. I have continued doing tasks that I didn't need to because I was unable to delegate them and I battled, in my day-to-day, against the grain.

What changed was my view on the world, the way I looked at my business and the commitment I made to myself to change it in spite of any obstacles. Through this process of strategic problem solving, implementation and on track management, I have empowered hundreds of clients to do the same and implement change to give them time to work ON the business, not IN the business, get paid what they are worth, take time away on holidays and have accountable and reliable staff.

My days now look like this:

I start my day with movement and reflection, a long walk with my dog and do some mindfulness exercises. When I get home, I make breakfast and have a lovely cup of coffee and chat with my love. At around 10am, I start working. I check in with my team, answer some emails and have a few client calls. Then I have a late lunch, a few more calls and call it a day at 4pm latest... time to go out again, get some fresh groceries and explore the city, where we meet up with friends and have a drink at a terrace before slowly returning home to prepare dinner. Cooking and having guests over for dinner is my biggest joy. The planning, preparation and cooking itself relaxes me.

Let me let you in on a little secret here... How I run my business is how I run my kitchen. I mastered the art of planning, leading, productivity, prosperity and REST from observing the professional kitchen. It is wildly known that professional cuisine is a tough, performance driven industry. However, it is also the most professional, well-organised industry I have seen in all my life. So, what does this have to do with RESTING,

RECEIVING, and running a Life and Business...well everything.

But it has not always been like this... I burned out TWICE before I gave myself a break and I stopped doing it all by myself. By allowing others to take care of things, trusting things would work out (often even better than I ever might have imagined), my life (and business) changed.

MY NEAR MISS BURNOUT(S).

I have always been a hard worker - not a hard worker as in breaking the overtime bank, but I love to give my all when it is about something or someone I care about.

I grew up as the youngest of three siblings. I was a late-comer and had 16 and 18 years of difference with my brothers. I was 18 months when we moved abroad, and my brothers moved out soon after. I had a happy childhood, despite my dad being away a lot due to his job in the military and my mom having her own troubles and coping mechanisms. This meant that I was alone a lot and had to take care of myself from an early age on. At the time, I was OK with it. Our house bordered to a large meadow with cows. These were my friends, my playing buddies. Whenever I wanted to play, or felt lonely or sad, I crawled under the fence to see my cow friends. As a child, I loved my time alone. It taught me to handle things on my own and to solve situations and problems that arose. I did not need help, I was like Pippi Longstocking... I could take on the world! I fully embraced this belief (and little Nadine did look like Pippi as well). My ability to manage things is a skill I took with me into adulthood and it has served me well (but not always).

I was, as I lovingly call it, an average overachiever who loved to wing it. The kind of person that does everything well, just a bit more than enough, but not going all the way. I dare to say I am a bit lazy, and when things don't have my interest, I really cannot be bothered. This is also how I navigated a big part of my career; if things sparked my attention, I jumped in with both feet, did the job brilliantly until I got bored and started looking for the next challenge. I am multi-passionate, which led to a patchwork–portfolio career as well. But hey, go with the flow and do what lights you up, right? Well, yes... if you listen to that inner voice and follow your intuition, but not if you do what you think you should do, according to what others believe you should. Such as following a certain career path. After I finished my studies – 2 studies in 5,5 years, including an exchange semester in South Korea (hello, overachiever!), I was ready for the BIG

CAREER. I knew I was able to pull off things in a short time that others thought were impossible, so I ended up in coordinating and big project managing roles. Tight deadlines and mad expectations. Whatever people threw at me I was able to bring it to an end, no problem. Is this all you got?!

I really appreciate this strength of mine, although it became my Achilles heel more than once. After several years climbing the corporate ladder, I found myself working as a leadership consultant for a large agency in Germany. I had recently moved to Munich from the Netherlands after having made redundant due to the 2008 economic crisis - an opportunity my partner and I embraced and took the jump to move to the city we both fell in love with a few years earlier. We settled in quite fast. He was on the road a lot due to his job and I had a stressful job in a fast-pacing organisation where I travelled a lot too, worked late and dealt with project specs that felt like they changed every 15 minutes. It was the lifestyle I chose and I was happy with, or I thought I was. I was, among others, responsible for a client project where we rolled out a large retail brand launch across seven countries simultaneously, with almost no budget, time or resources. A lot of fires to put out day in, day out and strings to pull to keep the project moving forward. Looking back, it was a recipe for disaster. And yes, disaster happened indeed, but not how you think.

One day, I woke up and could not move. My whole back was cramped. I had a dislocated disc a few years before, so all my alarms went off...no, not again... I decided to go to the doctor's, thinking I would get a painkiller so my muscles would relax again and I could get back to work quickly, 'cause they needed me, right? My doctor had other ideas... I remember sitting in her exam room and she looked at me intensely and asked me 'How are you REALLY doing, Ms de Zoeten?'. That was it. I cracked. I cried and told her I was miserable I was, under constant pressure and feeling like I could not breath most of the time. Just exhausted and sapping myself empty. That moment I realised how much I really hated my job and how much I was draining myself. My doctor wrote a sicknote for me for two weeks. Back home, I called my manager. She was not pleased and scolded me for endangering the project. I felt like a failure and beat myself up; It is not that difficult; I'd pulled off bigger projects in the past... why can I not finish this job? But my body made it clear: You stay right here and REST!

Three days later, the doorbell rang. There was a courier at the door who handed me an envelope. I opened it, it said I was fired. Are you friggin' kidding me? I am sick because of you and you are firing me? That moment was surreal and now that I write about it, I see the whole scene in front of my eyes again. But what I remember best, is how I felt. You know the valley of grief, where if you get bad news, you go through certain phases like shock, anger, denial, acceptance, hope and opportunity. Well, I did that whole rollercoaster in about three minutes. Yes, of course I was livid at my – now former – employer putting me aside like a piece of trash that easily. But at the same time, I was also relieved and this taught me three things:

1. Everyone is replaceable. It is not about me and there are others who can take care of business. I don't need to be superwoman everywhere;
2. My body and soul already knew for a while that I was not aligned with what I really wanted - always listen to your gut; and
3. I could now finally do what I really wanted: start my own business. Drop the expectations of others and do it my way.

So, I started my own leadership and team coaching and consultancy practice. I had a flying start from the beginning, landed a big deal with Microsoft Germany within a week of starting the business. I absolutely loved my business and what I did. I got to work with Fortune 500 companies and their leadership teams, travelled around Europe and met the most interesting and inspiring personalities. I decided when I wanted to work and with whom... at least that is what I thought. After a while, the glamor of the jet setting and hanging out with executives started to wear off. When I was home, I needed to divide myself between admin, client acquisition, my partner, raising a puppy, being a friend, daughter, kitchen queen etc. Money was good, I was paid well for my expertise, but something was missing...Freedom. Did I just create myself another job?

Three years into the business, I felt more and more out of control, tired, and exhausted. I was my business so I had to do it all, do the coaching, develop the programs and deliver them and when not onsite at a client's, I was chained to the computer to get everything else done. Never did I give myself a moment for myself. My health and work started to go down. The well-known darkness from my first burnout said hello again. One evening, after having delivered a workshop at a client's, I was sitting at the airport on my way back home. Of course, the plane was delayed, and this meant I had to ask my friends if my dog could stay another night with them. While texting with my friend (who was of course more than willing to take care of my puppy for another night) I burst into tears in the middle of the airport. A posh business man in a suit handed me a handkerchief (who said gentlemen were extinct??) and said: 'I don't know what you are going through, but remember: you always have a choice and help is there when you ask for it'. He smiled and disappeared to another gate. On the plane back home, I made a decision and this was the turning point. I started my business because I wanted freedom and live on my terms - not to be self-employed and my own worst boss. Then and there, I decided that if I wanted to live the life I want, I needed to stop doing what I always did: trying to do it all on my own and trying to do how everyone else is doing it. I have been the helper, the good girl, for way too long and now it was time for ME. I needed to step up as a CEO, a business owner. But how? I was just too exhausted. I was steering full speed into burnout number two.

After I came back home – and received a lot of doggie cuddles - I did what a lot of people in my shoes would not have dared. I STOPPED. I stopped everything. I cancelled my client engagements; I put my business on ice and got a job.

Wait, what???? I thought you wanted to live on your terms and live the dreamlife and you took up another job? Working for someone else?

Yes, I did. I needed a hard RESET; to stop running in circles, being worried and tired all the time about all the responsibilities that came with being self-employed. I was in desperate need of a break. One to think, to plan, in order to build a BUSINESS that supported my vision and my dream lifestyle. To become a CEO. See the distinction I made there between SELF EMPLOYED and CEO? I needed time to build my business up again, but this time, the right way. Taking up a job in a large corporation was a deliberate decision for several reasons: I could rest and recharge, earn money and pay my bills while cooking up my plan. Another reason to go back working for a boss was that I endured a big financial setback that had created a big debt, so I could not afford taking time off from business without generating income – but that story is for another time. My new job, as a senior HR/Leadership consultant, was fully in my line of expertise and gave me unique insiders insight of what is required to build a business that runs like clockwork.

During my time in the office, I did something I had not done in years as a solopreneur: working in teams and leading one. I had taught team-building and communication, especially in a remote setting, for years, but ironically, I was not part of one myself. Since I started my own business., everything relied on me; my business was me, myself and I. Because of my 'I've got it!' mentality, I found it hard to ask for help, to delegate and to hire… and for what? The exhaustion, sleepless nights, regular back issues, low on energy, weight gain, always on the gogogogo, being fully present… it was not worth it. It was the reason why I created such a mess in my business and life. It had to change, and I had to change. I needed start to ask for help, to lead, to rest, to receive. I needed to start walking my talk. You know the saying… slow down to accelerate. And this is literally what happened.

My RESET was my rescue and slowly, things started to unfold and to fall in place. I needed to learn how to take care and lead myself first, to rebuild my business. In 2019, I relaunched my business. This time I did something different. I put the foundations in place first: operations, systems and getting a team of people to help me.

As I mentioned before, my business is like a professional kitchen. Every task, every thing, every person has a certain place, role and order. Operations is key. Not sales, not marketing, not a fancy font on your website, not how many followers you have on Instagram. In order to grow a sustainable business and live a limitless life, you need to have your business backside in order. I know, not the sexy business talk you wanted to hear from me. Yet, I see too many entrepreneurs stuck at a certain level because they focus on the wrong things first, which leads to chaos, burnout and standstill. Like putting the donkey behind the chariot. Leading a business is about leadership and order.

LEADERSHIP

Let's talk about leadership. When you think of leadership many will think of public figures like Obama, Oprah or Gandhi, or the gazillion in a box corporate leadership programmes. Not directly something you think of as a small business owner. Yet leadership, especially self-leadership is what makes or breaks a business. You are a leader the moment you decide to start your business. You want to make a difference. Entrepreneurship is about leading; leading yourself, leading others and leading impact. The place many business owners feel inadequate is, in their ability to lead others, especially their team.

Being a solopreneur is all about being the leader of ONE.

You.

On your own, you can be a successful person. But not a successful leader.

As a solopreneur, our agenda is all about helping ourselves and to a certain extent others. Running the business by ourselves and earning money while doing what we love. But, we only can come so far on our own. And usually solopreneurs (with some exceptions) get stuck at a certain income and impact level when they get maxed out.

As a company owner, you have more opportunities to grow. However, this requires a shift - as John Maxwell calls it, "Leadershift". In his book, Leader Shift, he gives the example of going from soloist to conductor. A solo musician can pick up their instrument and play whenever they want, for as long as they want, and can play whichever song they want. On the other hand, a conductor can't do that. She must be on other people's schedules. She must take into consideration the abilities and personalities of a group of people, she must communicate her vision, and in the end, she's responsible for their success or failure as an orchestra. Can you imagine a solo musician all of a sudden becoming a conductor and what shifts they must make so that the entire orchestra works as one incredible unit to accomplish limitless possibilities?!?

When I began growing my own team, ALL of my insecurities and self-limiting beliefs came rushing to the surface.

My need for approval.

My need to be liked and loveable.

My need to never show a shred of weakness or that I wanted help.

My need to please other people so no one would get mad at me or think about me in a negative way.

The behaviour I developed as a high achiever was the ability to work alone and be incredibly proficient and quite excellent at everything.

BUT...

Ultimately, doing it all alone had led to exhaustion, stress, and burnout.

I became very aware of this type of pattern in myself when I ran my first business. It made me pause my business and go back to corporate.

Like each of us who are dedicated to personal growth even more than external goals, I started working with a mentor, whose expertise is in communication.

Clearly, the way I was communicating with MYSELF wasn't effective and I was AVOIDING communicating with other people to ASK FOR HELP.

One time, I was at an event with this new mentor where we had a group discussion on how we "recruit" people in our lives. At first, I didn't quite understand the question when I was asked, "Nadine, how do you recruit people?" (Meaning how do you "influence" people to do something for you.).

Because I paused for a few too many seconds, my mentor asked another participant in the room, "How does Nadine recruit people?"

The man said, "Well, she puts a smile on her face and she's nice and she's pretty and she doesn't clearly state what she wants her outcomes to be to that person."

Nailed it.

He was right. I was way to wishy washy and nice to others and did not clearly say want I wanted and expected from others.

The BIG lesson I learned through that exchange was that I had an opportunity to "recruit" people in a much stronger, bolder, more precise, and instructing way.

And that was really good news.

So, where did this type of behaviour and communication pattern in me originate?

From a very young age and then into adulthood, I felt unsafe to clearly state what I wanted.

I would run my thoughts through these filters before speaking:

"What if someone doesn't like me because of what I want, my boundaries, or what's important to me?"

"What if I push people away because I'm too bold or what I believe doesn't align with their beliefs or opinions?"

"What if I push someone else's trigger buttons and then I have to deal with conflict or confrontation?"

Growing up, I had a dad who was away a lot and a mom who was emotionally unavailable. When we were all together, we made sure we had a good time and didn't talk about bad things. Confrontation was not something we lovingly practiced. We brushed things under the carpet.

As a very young child I decided, "When you communicate it hurts people, they get mad, and/or they don't like you because of what you say when you open your mouth."

What I've realized in my adult years (yes finally) is that it's not that I was afraid of people or confrontation, it's that I didn't have very much practice in communicating what I wanted with other people. As a child, communicating didn't lead to good things. Therefore, I didn't practice it. I avoided it at all costs. And would end up resentful, down the road, with the dynamic in relationships I'd created.

For years I always felt like a strong, competent, clear, and quite bold leader.

On the inside.

But, on the outside I came across as nice, smiley, lovely, people pleasing, and the "Yes Woman".

That way of operating was probably one of the reasons why I was such a successful "Team Player" in corporate for years. I never took up a role as a leader, I preferred to play the role of "the woman behind the woman." Or the "objective consultant" is that who I was? Is that what I really wanted?

No way. And I changed it. I stepped into my own version of what leadership is. I decided to step up, be seen and be fully me. But this was not easy. I had to leave my safe comfort zone and erase old patterns in order to become the 2.0. version of Nadine. Nadine the leader, calm, confident, well rested and kind.

The decision to stop my consulting business to get a job, and later relaunching my business all over again, was one of the most excruciating experiences of my entire life.

I was afraid of letting people I loved down, letting my business down, letting the clients down, letting myself down.

I was afraid to say out loud what I really wanted for my own life, regardless of what anyone thought about my decision or of me.

It was absolutely a breakthrough moment for me.

As you can imagine, when I brought on team members literally overnight in 2019, many of those same insecurities resurfaced.

The next level of radical growth activated many of those same insecurities in me.

This time, as the leader of my own team and growing company, there was no more hiding or pretending.

Leadership and team building has become a passion and obsession of mine in the past couple of years. And there is a big difference between teaching how to lead (as I did as a leadership consultant) and being a leader myself.

It was the learning curve of all learning curves.

More than anything, I've recognized that in order for us to bring our big, bold, ambitious visions to the world, we need a team of people surrounding us.

And that team deserves a leader who will train, coach, manage, and LEAD them. When we shift from solopreneur to visionary leader, we get to focus on others to bring out their best - to help others reach their individual and team potential. Sow seeds of value into your people and you will receive a harvest of unexpected blessings. Lean in and trust that things will work out. Let go of control and doing it all by yourself.

REST & RECEIVE

Let me ask you a question: can your company run without you?

It's a simple question with a "yes" or "no" answer.

Yet, most entrepreneurs struggle to answer this question. If you're like most entrepreneurs, you answered "no." After all, you say, you're successful because you found a massive problem and solved it. You are your company, and your company is you. Right?

Wrong.

All wrong.

Why you ask?

Let me answer your question with a few questions.

- Are you looking for true success and fulfilment?
- Interested in growing (or even selling) your company for 7/8-figures, or more?
- Would you like to stop the daily grind so you can work on your business and not in it?

If you answered "yes" to any of the above questions, you MUST have a company that runs without you. This might sound counterintuitive, but if you want to create true wealth and freedom in your business, you need to start working less. You get to let people support you in your business and you need to give up control over doing everything yourself. You have to embrace elimination, automation and delegation. Too much focus on effort can have the opposite effect – we can get bogged down in procrastination, over complication and resistance to delegating.

But what if it can be easier? What if you could create a business in a way that worked perfectly for you without feeling like you're paddling upstream? It is possible. Remember, it does not mean you'll never have to work, like Denise Duffield Thomas says in her book 'Chill-preneur': 'Business isn't effort-none but it can be effort-less.'

Set your priorities first and plan the rest around it. Two of my personal heroes are Sarah Blakeley and Jesse Itzler. Both are highly successful entrepreneurs, yet, if you follow them on Instagram, all you will see is that they put their family life (which is sometimes hilarious but heart-warming) as the number one priority. As Jesse puts it in his words: 'My kids only have one youth, I will never be too tired to play for them, I make them a priority.' I love how he has his 'Big Ass Calendar', literally an A3 wall calendar that he carries around wherever he goes. He plans family time, personal development, and other priorities dear to his heart first and THEN, only then, everything else.

When it comes to running a successful business, I work with my R.E.S.T framework. I apply it with my clients, and I have built my own business on these foundations. It goes as follows:

R – Rest & Routines = Results – Take care of yourself first and set priorities, create daily routines in business and life and focus on what brings in the results.

E – Energy -What gives you energy and what drains you? Use this as your compass on what you should focus on and what not (and delegate to others). Be aware of what energy type you are, we are all designed differently. What works for me does not work for you.

S – Simple, sustainable systems – Keep it simple. Don't overcomplicate things in your business, if you can't explain it to your 7 Y/O nephew or your 70 Y/O Mom in a few sentences, you need to go back to the drawing board. Systemise what is possible and automatise as well. Don't reinvent the wheel and standardize the operations in your company. Remember what I told you earlier about the professional kitchen? How everything has a reason, place, order and role? Do that.

T – Team and Time Mastery. Being relentless about your time is essential. Schedule your priorities first and then the rest. Personal priorities come before meetings. Team − If you want to grow your business to something that is beyond you, having support is not an option. It is a requirement.

I made **FREEDOM** in business non-negotiable. Taking a step back to rest and creating a structured business is what got my life back. I created a business that runs for me, not by me. I have a dedicated team that is close knit and often acts as my second brain, reminding me of all the stuff and running the business without me so that have the bandwidth to focus on what lights me up, whether that is another project, mentoring others, speaking, or like now, contributing to a book for trailblazing, liberty-loving entrepreneurs like you.

These days I can take time off whenever I want, work no more that 4- 6 hours a day, 4 days a week and 44 weeks a year. I took the busy out of business and created freedom. I made it my life work to stop entrepreneurial burnout by helping entrepreneurs to grow a business that is not only profitable and financially strong, but also supports their life goals and enables their Joie de Vivre. I absolutely love my work, and nothing makes me happier than seeing business owners stepping up as leaders and become CEOs... CEOs of their business and of their lives. To spend more time with their loved ones, inspire their teams

and clients, be fulfilled, full of energy and indulging in
the simple, luxurious things of life while having a business that runs like clockwork.

If you want to take your business to the next level,
grow to multiple six-figures, and eventually to your
own seven-figure business, without sacrificing your life,
my team and I can help you do this by teaching you
about systems, hiring the right support, delegating
better, shifting your business model and role in the
business so your company works with more clients,
while you work less and REST more. You can literally
Sleep and Grow Rich...by having your business do the
heavy work, take a step back, rest and be the wealthy
powerful CEO of your life and business.

ABOUT THE AUTHOR

NADINE DE ZOETEN

Nadine de Zoeten is a leadership mentor, business psychologist and wealth advocate for ambitious business leaders who want to do Big Business with ease.

She is the founder and CEO of the S.L.E.E.P. and Grow Rich Institute, business and leadership institute specialised in equipping overwhelmed 6-figure entrepreneurs to design a business and team that can run like clockwork and reach 7 figures without sacrificing their lives.

She has worked with countless business leaders – from micro-businesses to Fortune 500 companies – to streamline their systems, simplify their processes, coach teams and leaders, and create strategic growth while cutting costs, saving time, and expanding their profit margins.

She is extremely passionate about helping business women become their wealthiest selves, be recognised as the top of their industries and live a life on their terms, without exhaustion. When not helping her clients from all over the world become great leaders and creating a freedom lifestyle by having a 5 star business, she explores Europe in her campervan, aka, her 'office on wheels'.

She fully embodies the #Work from Anywhere philosophy, not only in her own business but also by teaching her clients how to achieve this.

Nadine absolutely loves to roam French markets in order to find the best ingredients to cook lovely dinners for friends.

She is an avid collector of cookbooks – especially Italian or French. Nadine's current homebase is Munich where she lives with her husband and cute pup.

Nadine is available for leadership & team development projects, as well as private consultations and coaching.

You can reach Nadine at:

Email - hello@nadinedezoeten.com.

Website - www.nadinedezoeten.com

facebook.com/nadine.dezoeten

instagram.com/nadinedezoeten

linkedin.com/in/nadinedezoeten

NICOLE THORNE

PERMISSION TO EXERCISE YOUR WAY!

*W*hen this book hits the shelves, I will be 49 years old and I will have been in the fitness industry for 30 years. What a trip it has been! In this time I have re-invented myself several times to be who I am today. Where I started from is literally the exact opposite of who I am today in every aspect.

Today I am an extremely proud mother of two strong, independent and amazing teenage girls. They are both very active and driven and I can't wait to see where their futures take them. I run my own company called Nicole Thorne Fitness, also known as Pelvic Floor Secrets on my social media channels. I am on a mission to inform every woman on the planet that there are answers as to why their bodies are in pain, why they struggle with incontinence (leaking) and why they just don't feel great. I want them all to know that it is not difficult to implement small changes that will turn their health around. I take extreme pleasure in educating and teaching on this topic and use the hashtag #changinglives because that is what I do on a daily basis.

When women reach out to me for help it is usually because they have tried all of the things they are told to but have not yet found their way. I help them find their way and overcome the loathing they feel for fitness once and for all. There is a very specific reason people do not like fitness, or at least think they don't like it. It is because they were never taught or shown how to implement a proper foundation. The basics, starting with the center of their body, were missing. They have never been taught about the core. This is the fundamental part of the body where everything starts - vitality or pain.

When this foundation is not taught or built, women end up hurting themselves either acutely or slowly over time. Further to this, people like to jump in and try to change everything all at once. This very rarely works. Their body knows it and forces them to quit, leaving them to think fitness is not for them. I have heard stories like this from many clients over the years. After working with one client in particular for 3 months, she shared that she had hired other trainers several times, but working with me was the first time that she was not injured at the 3 month mark.

The trouble you are having in the fitness world is not your fault, it is just the way fitness is delivered and has been delivered for a very long time. It does not help that the media is also extremely confusing to boot, making you feel like there is no way you can conquer your fitness goals. A goal which I wholeheartedly believe everyone wants. They just haven't found their way yet. This is my gift; showing people the way to exercise their way, enjoy and look forward to it.

When I started in the fitness world, I was 19 years old, just starting my first year at university and I was ready to conquer the world! I thought the way to present fitness to the world was through exercise classes and weight loss marketing. Truth be told, I was a regular shaped girl, not particularly overweight, yet I loathed my body from a very early age. I can remember doing Jane Fonda exercise videos in my basement as early as 13 years old. I worked very hard trying to alter my body. However, looking back, I now know that though I had youth on my side, what I was doing would never give me the body aesthetics I so desired.

It was the nineties, a time when we did cardio and cardio type workouts along with eating as little as possible to try and get the results we were after. Women all over the world are still doing this. I know this to be true because I talk to them every day and they tell me so. Particularly women my age and older. This strategy does not work! Not only does it make you miserable and just looking forward for it to end, but you just cannot change your body doing this, period! What you will end up with is a wrecked metabolism, less lean muscle mass (the very thing you need to support your body), cause havoc for your poor hormones and oh, did I say live a miserable life? Is it any wonder nine out of ten women I interview say they hate exercise and fitness!

If there is one thing I would like you to get from my experience it is: this is NOT the way to succeed! You CAN exercise YOUR way, enjoy it and have it fit easily into your life without sacrificing the things you love, all while getting the results you so desire. The results I love seeing the most are women living in pain- and leak-free bodies, having strength to enjoy the people and life they love, and yes, aesthetics can be part of that too. Personally, I look at aesthetics as a really awesome bonus. When my fitness journey started all those years ago, these goals were not on my radar and my choice of fitness modality (classes) would never have gotten me to them anyhow. It has taken me many years to figure this out and now I am so lucky to get to share it with women every day!

The way to having a pain-free, strong and confident body is to learn the basics, or as I like to call them, the foundations first. You need to start slow, take it one step at a time, strength train with intention, teaching your body to make your foundation training automatic and natural. This is the way to heal your body all day every day. There is no rush. You have lived in your current body for 40, 50, maybe 60 years plus so let's pick the sustainable road and make the results you get those you get to keep for life, not just a few weeks.

The way I was doing things before was not serving me or the people coming to me. Now I get to make actual, sustainable, amazing changes to people's lives. I feel that after 30 years of continuous learning and pivoting, I have arrived where I am supposed to be and I am doing what I was always meant to do. The learning and pivoting never ends; if you stop learning and changing you will be left behind as things evolve and grow. I am excited to be part of growth every step of the way. It makes for a bright future.

Would I speak to my younger self and change everything if I could? No, I would not. I realize I had to go through those steps to have the knowledge and experience I do now. Without these experiences, I would not have the depth of knowledge and offerings that I do today.

My very first job in the fitness world was teaching group fitness classes at my local YMCA community center. This is where I took my first certification course and then started to volunteer as a group fitness instructor. Not too long after that, in 1991, I applied and tried out to teach fitness classes at my University. I got the job! I was so excited to have my first paying job in fitness, that came with a whopping $10 per class pay cheque! To say I loved it would be the understatement of the century. I loved every moment, even when I had to get up early after staying up all night partying with my friends (guys, it was University, my first time away from home). I had my share of getting up with a severe headache and still showing up for my participants with energy, loud music and a smile.

Yay for our early twenties, right?

Teaching here was as close to feeling like a rock star as I am going to get. Our classes had hundreds of energetic early twenties participants jumping too fast, high energy music. I got to stand on a large podium and have two hundred plus young adults follow my every move.

I remember one time at the end of the class feeling my adrenaline so high, I actually got mixed up for a moment thinking I was on stage performing a rock concert. A few years later, still in my undergrad, I got the job as assistant coordinator for the entire fitness program team. I was beaming with pride and took this very seriously. At the time I felt convinced this was going to be my path, and I was going to make coordinating a fitness team my career.

After University, I moved to Toronto, a major metropolitan city in my country, Canada, to start my new life in this exciting city. I soon learned that teaching classes was not enough to pay my bills, however I was very determined to make a go of it so I started waiting tables on the side to make ends meet. I was living the life, living with my boyfriend (now my husband) in one of the most vibrant cities in the world, young and teaching at a beautiful luxury gym chain called (at the time) Sports Clubs of Canada. Oh, but still having to waitress so I could pay my rent. Back then I never touched a weight higher than 5lbs. Pretty different from the hundreds of pounds I lift now!

Although I am genetically very blessed with a hard working, strong Dutch body, I started feeling the effects of this busy lifestyle. I was teaching multiple classes per day, so you would think I was ultra healthy, but this in fact was not the case. I felt tired all the time and had a flu or cold pretty much at least once per month. I did not listen or realize it, but my body was giving me hints and trying to tell me:hey this is not the way, not sustainable and although you are having fun, let's maybe seek an alternative path, eh? Still, I did not connect the dots. The thing is, I did not yet have the life experience. That life experience is what has now taught me what does work for sustainability, strength and getting the healthy body I was aiming for myself and my clients.

Around 1996 or so, I started to dabble in the personal training world, but boy, did I have a lot to learn!I was fortunate to be learning from many different types of disciplines, from bodybuilding experts to elite athlete trainers, in addition to my own experiences. Learning I did and as I said before this never stops. I imagine in every industry this is probably the case, but in fitness for sure if you stop learning you do not stay up to date and get stale and left behind pretty fast. I have to admit at first I trained people illegitimately, what I mean is, I was not even certified yet. The fitness world can be like the wild west. Most of you would have some personal experience with this statement I am sure. I actually did not get officially certified as a personal trainer until a few years in. You could say I went to the school of real life. I will be forever grateful for the wide variety of training styles I got to be exposed to. This allowed me to blend my true calling of blending pelvic floor rehab and strength training into the systems I use to help my clients today.

When I first learned about the pelvic floor I had no idea how life changing it would be but I would eventually learn and put it all together. I continued learning through courses, my peers with more experience, and also what was happening to my own body as I went through various life stages. I would apply various fitness modalities to myself all along the way and I would watch myself and my clients change or not change depending on the modality that I chose.

After I had my first daughter at 34 years old (2006), I started calling myself a "postnatal trainer." Knowing what I know now, this was not a true statement, rather I was a trainer that had babies. However I am thankful I did this because it opened the doors for me to meet the very people who helped me fix my own postnatal issues and get me to where I am today with the knowledge, experience and passion to help hundreds of women find their way with fitness.

At this time I was a new mom myself so my focus was very much the young moms, who had just had babies. I was obsessed with abdominal separation (Diastasis Recti) and later the pelvic floor. My focus was the newly postnatal woman. However as I became older, my clients aged with me and now my favourite clientele is the woman mid forties and above. I love this demographic because I feel that we aged in a world where fitness was, well...crap, with endless misinformation or lack of information. We were working so hard but hitting our heads against the wall choosing modalities that were not helping us, but in fact getting us injured and technically fatter as we lost lean muscle mass the more we did it.

I now get to be the person who changes these women's lives. How fun and exhilarating is that? I will forever be grateful for the steps and people that got me to this point. Every step of the way a new coach presents him or herself to me and it allows me to take the next leap forward. I feel proud to be that person with the strength to understand that I do not know it all, I am open to learn and ask for help and admit I have changed as I've found better ways. I would hate to still be in the same mind and place that I was when I started at 19 years of age. It was great at the time and gives me experience that now gives me empathy and understanding of what my clients have gone through too.

Today I realize although I have many certifications, this helps and is necessary of course, this is not what makes you good at your craft. What makes you good is the hundreds of case studies, being in the trenches doing the reps as they say, the countless stumbles, and wrong turns, the endless learning and pivoting along the way. This is what makes you who you are; this cannot be rushed, it takes what it takes.

Honestly people flock to me because of my age and experience. It is something that can only be earned through time and being open and willing to learn. There is no way I could have showed up for people then, as I do today, as I had no idea what they were going through. I am grateful for every step, and although I have felt frustrated at times because I have given many hours of time and free labour I realize now it was actually free learning, not the other way around. It was certainly worth it.

Something profound that happened to me in this journey was getting injured after having my babies. The information and support available to women after having babies is pretty much non-existent. Even though I had been a fitness trainer/instructor for over 15 years when I had my babies, I had never even heard the term pelvic floor, never mind knowing what I had to do to help me protect it. Even after taking a pre and postnatal national certifications, I still never heard this major anatomical muscle and fundamental part of our bodies mentioned. This is where we were as an industry, still are, but getting better slowly. Thank goodness!

After I had my daughters, the task I assigned myself was get my body back and stat! I felt very strongly at the time that if anyone could do it quickly it would be me, a fitness professional afterall. Well this is the only time I will say that a sedentary person may have been better off than me.

I worked out very hard and dieted equally as stringently. I did not put two and two together when I had debilitating back pain to the point that I could not lift my infant out of her crib to take care of her, and leaking to the point that some days I could not leave my house. Not life threatening but VERY life altering.

Let me remind you I was a mid thirty year old woman with 2 young daughters. Yes, my body looked incredible and an envy for many, but what good was that to me? I could literally not live my life without being panicked that I smelled like pee or be in such pain that I could not easily move my body that I had spent my entire adult life taking the best care of that I could.

Now, as annoying and painful as this was, I would not be the trainer I am today if it wasn't for this important life lesson learned the hard way. I was super lucky to have met the right people who led me to the answers to reverse the damage I had caused my body (in the name of trying to better it, I might add). This part was not a swift and fast process. It was dripped to me in tiny parts over a 5 or more year period, in fact, heck, I am still learning as the research itself is evolving every single year. I am lucky to call several amazing physiotherapists my friends who have and still help me along the way.

However, during this time I worked on myself and started helping the women who entrusted their health to me, all the while building up my confidence in myself to allow me to start public speaking and allowing myself to show up more publicly in general.

This took time. I was scared to death of being judged and challenged. I remembered being mortified if something came up that I did not know the answers to. Then one day I realized the smartest physicians and surgeons do not know every single thing with the human body. It was ok to ask for help on things I did not know, while allowing myself to speak loudly and clearly about the life changing things I do know and know very well.

This was a pivotal, very empowering moment in my life and career. No one knows it all, practice your scope, learn continuously and don't hold back. People need you! Once I allowed myself to step into this, everything changed. It's not easy putting yourself out there especially in an ever changing landscape like the fitness world, but it is worth it and necessary to fly, but most importantly to leave a wake of changed humans behind you. It has happened more than once that a person had a body ailment that was significantly affecting their life, and I was able to help them while their surgeon could not.

The surgeon could operate (which is definitely not my scope) but the after care, core and body strengthening and mobilizing was out of their scope but most certainly in mine and it gives me great pleasure to offer this to people.

Most recently I met a woman 65 years old living in constant pain and feeling very unhappy, upset and desperate for help. The year before, she underwent major abdominal surgery to remove a part of her intestine. After, she was told that she had Diastasis Recti separation (abdominal separation that happens vertically on the body) but her surgery was horizontal.

She was not given any education or information that a horizontal cut could never cause a vertical separation, her diastasis Recti if she had it, she had that since she gave birth to her babies 40 plus years ago. However with no information what does a person do? They fear the worst; she thought her body might burst open if she wasn't careful, so she literally curled herself into a forward ball in order to protect herself (not an uncommon situation). She had immense pain.

When she came to me we solved these things in a very short time, I educated her and gave her permission to open her chest (stretch it) along with my other modalities, and she felt better right away. She told me that she also felt that her organ or something in her body felt like it was falling when she laid on one side. After contemplating this for a bit, I realized this might be a similar situation as a woman undergoing a hysterectomy. The removal of the uterus leaves a space that other organs can now fall into if the core is not functioning as it should. Since her appointment with her surgeon to check on this issue was later that month, we proceeded.

I always recommend to start or continue strengthening regardless of appointments because you will have to do this regardless of the future outcomes, then I always say, let's see if this handles the issue in the meantime. Guess what; it did!! It usually does. She did get her appointment and unfortunately the surgeon knew nothing about this (nor is strengthening necessarily their scope) however she literally told my client that she was wasting her time talking about her trainer and program. This is unfortunate but in the meantime my client is getting better so all is good, but what about the women that are not so lucky and are in this boat receiving this incorrect information about their bodies and quality of life.

So now my mission has shifted to being a loud educator and informant for women everywhere. You must advocate for yourself, seek second, third, even fourth opinions if necessary. My core training saves, this I know and have experienced over and over again. However my delivery of the information was very slow because my main delivery choice was one on one in person personal training. I realized this had to change. I could at least build an online course to give women the information of what to do to protect their core and body and apply it themselves to their choice of workout. This could be anything from strength training (my preferred modality), to yoga, gardening or simply taking care of their children. In January of 2020 I had this information filmed and compiled. This was the first step in another huge shift in my business and my reach for helping women. Little did I know everything was about to change drastically with the entire world including the fitness space.

Enter COVID-19. We all had to close our facilities. Armed with my foundation program newly filmed, I launched it on the day that we were officially locked down as an entire province. I had the time now to focus and gain confidence with my online offerings; we had no choice, but for me, it was the right amount of pressure to get me to take huge leaps forward.

As my confidence grew, my results online were giving me more and more reassurance to continue on this path. I started realizing I could never help the number of women I want to help by continuing my one by one approach. On a daily basis, I am faced with individuals telling me about their body issues and mistreatment in our current health spaces. I wanted to find a way to grow my reach, however previously I had a lot of doubt about my ability to manage technology in order to make my vision a reality. I started to look outside of myself to help me reach new heights that I knew were possible. I have literally had 2-3 coaches at any given time, the past while. The same as I expect the woman in pain to reach out to me and tap into my years of knowledge and experience to help themselves, I had to apply this to my business.

Getting closer to 50 years old and my kids becoming more and more independent each day, it was time for massive action. Every coach brings another angle to my life, all the angles that I am very thirsty for. I could not have done what I have done so far without each and every one of them. The in-roads I have made as of late with my online offerings are so exciting. I simply did not have this skill set to have technology and the internet take me as a friend. This fear of technology, social media and the internet as a whole was holding me back in a big way.

COVID taught me something very big, it forced me to take on this world, I did it sort of kicking and screaming at first I have to admit. I can proudly say that this is changing my business and life and the lives of the women I reach, for the better, one thousand fold, with each passing day. The changes I have made with my business pivoting to online and working at making my offerings feel as "in person as possible" started doubling my revenue last year and I am well on my way to doubling that again this year! I have to admit I used to think it was a lot cheaper to "do things yourself" and not seek help. Now, I don't think so. I spent years and years at a standstill with my business, making my reach and revenue very small, until I decided to take chances and get help. It's funny how you expand.

Take the first step and see your life change. This goes for business, health and your life in general. I am very aware now of my strengths and I want to focus on that, not knock my head against a wall trying to piece together things I do not understand.

People can hire me to help them with their bodies in a swift manner because of the years of sweat it took me to get to my current knowledge. Equally I can accept help from others too, who have done the same in the things I do not know. This is probably the most valuable lesson I have learned in the last few years. This revelation has changed things for me more than anything else I've learned. This says a lot based on the fact that learning the power of the pelvic floor and how it blends with strength training for miraculous results was a pretty big revelation too. In reality one could not exist without the other.

Now I spend my days talking to women, educating, bringing up awareness and teaching them that it is possible to change and it is not too late. I enjoy speaking to large crowds, delivering webinars and free training, and now writing a chapter in a book that is going to be spread all over the world (this from a girl who was gifted a grammar book as a teen because my grammar was apparently so bad) all in the name of education and spreading awareness. It is where change can start.

I have immensely enjoyed writing this chapter for you and I want to leave you with this; No one can be an expert at everything. Becoming specialized in an area takes a lot of effort, time and passion. If you try to dabble and be good at a variety of things you might not get to the outcome you might have hoped for. For me I will focus on my scope. This is not to say I won't expand my scope over time; I will, but I will not feel like I need to also be specialized at marketing, technology etc., too. This I can get help with and have people who are as specialized as I am in my scope do these portions for me for exponentially more growth.

This realization has changed my business and life like nothing else ever has. This allows the kind of growth that a few years ago I could not have even conceived of. I am very excited for the future, for the women that I will help who will continue to live more vibrant, pain and leak free lives, enjoying their children and grand-children and a healthy lifestyle that is a natural extension of themselves.

This is my dream: to have every woman be aware of what is happening to their bodies, how certain things may not be serving them even though they previously thought they were. They can learn their way and fall in love with a world I have been in love with my entire adult life, they can inspire their own children like I have and the fitness landscape can slowly change to be better for us all.

Let me leave you with this last thought: if your body is giving you hints, e.g., getting sick often, leaking, in pain etc, it is time to take action. Bodies are not meant to live in this type of state. There are solutions; these solutions are not yet mainstream, but you can help yourself as you help me let others know too.

Here is to healthier happier middle aged women all over the world.

ABOUT THE AUTHOR

NICOLE THORNE

Nicole Thorne is a strength training coach specializing in helping women eliminate leaking and pain by restoring their functional core system.

She is a Certified Fitness Professional, Master Trainer for Core Confidence Education (the leading certification for pre/postnatal rehabilitation), with over 30 years of experience training women.

She is also the owner of Nicole Thorne Fitness and the founder of Pelvic Floor Secrets.

She believes in retraining and resetting the body first and foremost so safe movement becomes natural and automatic, before embarking on strength training programs that meet women where they are in their own health and fitness journeys.

Women who have trained with Nicole rave about her programs, her motivating personality, and above all, the results they achieve!

She inspires women to reach their goals and to stop their declining health, through education and empowerment by ensuring each woman that she trains gets the results they crave without compromising their body.

You can find out more about my work and download my free core breath download by visiting my website www.nicolethornefitness.com

I can be reached at www.nicolethornefitness.com

Or join me in my free FB group called Pelvic Floor Secrets

https://www.facebook.com/groups/pelvicfloorsecrets

instagram.com/pelvic_floor_secrets

SERA JOHNSTON

PERMISSION TO BE YOU – UNLOCK THE
PERSON WITHIN.

*W*ho would have thought, looking back
on my journey from being a child at
school, to being a working mother, raising a child diagnosed with Cerebral Palsy at just 13 months old, that
one day, I'd be impacting women across the globe; I'd
be changing the way clinicians interact with parents,
and the best selling published author of two books...
that I'd be known as one of the top ten inspiring
women by Global Woman magazine?

I always knew I was different, never quite fitting in with
a particular group of kids at school or work colleagues,
yet I got on with everyone. I guess it's the Mediter-
ranean in me; with an Italian father and Spanish
mother, my upbringing was very *mi casa es su casa* (my
house is your house) - everyone welcome. I remember
fondly every Christmas Eve after attending midnight

mass, my father used to invite what seemed like the whole church back to our house for food and drinks, even the priest came – it was a tradition that carried on for many years. Although I have not continued the tradition, after my father passed away, I inherited his house, allowing me to refurbish and create a home I'm incredible proud of, keeping the original structure of the front lounge where most of the gatherings took place.

I get to live my life every day, making a difference to women's lives because I know what it means to rediscover the person within and lead a life on your terms – to be a non-conformist, have an inner belief and confidence within you that allows you to follow what's right for you regardless of any obstacles getting in the way.

Living a life of purpose aligned to my values enables me to tune in and listen to my gut, always knowing when something doesn't feel right and asking myself, what is this telling me? Having the freedom to travel around the world and experience different cultures brings joy not only to myself, but also to my children. Giving them the experience of seeing the world in real life for themselves allows the possibilities of endless opportunities for them. My son has set his intention of gaining a scholarship and studying in the USA; he has done his research and found the ideal university. I truly believe this is due to the life we lead today.

Letting go of things that I can't control has led to a meaningful and fulfilling life which has rippled across family and business. Stepping into my own power, deciding I am the author of my story and the leader of my life. Owning my future and not allowing others to dictate what that will look like. It's not about following the crowd just because others have done it a certain way. It's about doing it your way, without apologising, even if others don't agree. It's about having the right people around you – battery chargers not battery drainers. Your past doesn't define your future – would you drive your car looking in the rear-view mirror? When you change your mindset, your perception is different. Leading a fulfilling life is not stating every-thing is perfect and there are never challenges, of course there are. The difference is where I place my focus. I don't focus on what's missing or lacking, I focus on what I want and find a solution, a way to achieve it. I remember doing a vision board years ago. I came across it recently and every single picture has come true – from personal and business growth, how I wanted my house and garden to look and getting to fly first class.

When you set the intention and it so strongly aligned with who you are, you become unstoppable. There is a limitless number of possibilities. The only person standing in the way is you, because it only takes a moment for change to happen.

My daughter, who is now 22 and definitely no longer a child, is living her dream, having graduated with a Law degree and leading an independent life. A vast difference from a life of having all her needs met from birth and leading a solitary life, others doubting and ridiculed her dreams. She ignored the naysayers and I am so proud of everything she has accomplished so far, becoming an independent, confident young woman. I still have to pinch myself when she calls me on the phone for a chat, telling me all about her day. This was my biggest wish for her.

I remember my dad telling me as a child, when I leave school, get a good job working in a bank and I'd be set for life. I knew then I didn't want to be confined and had other ideas, yet, there was an underlining rule, a belief, that I truly believe was passed down by my parents, and that was to follow the rules, conform with the status quo, work hard and do a good job. Nothing about being aligned with your purpose, values and yourself. These didn't matter.

I knew I'd always wanted children and to continue working, build a home and have a family. I gave up on my true passion, as a hairdresser working for John Frieda, as the financial security of working for an insurance company allowed me and my now husband the opportunity to buy our first home. My parents were less pleased, as we were not married. Yet for us, we were on the property ladder. Deep down, I always felt I had let go of what I loved, what I was good at. I was top of the class, represented my college at regional hairdressing competitions. To then work for John Frieda was fabulous. But, that part of me was gone. I soon learnt how to become a chameleon, blending into the world of insurance and soon became a trainer. My creativity returned and I discovered I enjoyed training others. By this point, I had become a mother and after a year maternity leave, I returned to work. My life was going as planned; I got married, moved to a new house, started a family, my career was progressing well... But I was fitting into a mould which was not made for me. By working hard and doing a good job, I was ticking the right boxes – the organisational boxes. I was conforming to the expectation and going above and beyond. Coming up with new ideas to make service improvements, implementing these changes and seeing the results were a huge personal and professional boost, being noticed and validated. Yet at what cost?

The pattern continued when I moved into a management role within the NHS. I loved what I did - training and development, facilitating team development days and providing solutions in a consultancy capacity, in addition to people management. The more I gave my everything, the more validation I received. Always going further, finding a solution and being involved in the action, I felt unstoppable. I threw myself into my work, attending meeting after meeting, often eating lunch mid-afternoon. Becoming a mother – a working mother, I felt I could do it all and I did – until a curve ball came out of the blue that shook my world and pulled the rug from underneath me and everything I had known. My daughter was diagnosed with Cerebral Palsy aged just 13 months.

I believed what I was told by the doctors, especially the ones in Harley Street who I went to for a second opinion. Believed her prognosis. Believed everything her life would be, according to those who were medically trained. I followed the rules, because 'they' knew best, right? I could hear my parents say 'listen to the doctors, they know best'. Yet nobody could explain to me how one day my life was as I had planned, and the next day I was thrown into a world of disability, an alien world I had no experience of. A different language was spoken. This world was bleak, with no hope or future. If I did everything I was told, surely there was hope, but the message was loud and clear 'don't set high expectations'

The truth was, I did set high expectations for myself, for my daughter, and for the people I worked with. It was clear when it came to my daughter, I had a different vision for her future, one that was not a consideration in the medical, education and social world. I continued working in my management role, juggling work, hospital appointments and mothering responsibilities – I could do it all. My role providing the appropriate care, medical intervention, school assistance and all things disability related became another full-time job. I became consumed with 'getting the job done'. I no longer felt like a mother, I was detached emotionally when focused on the task in hand. I became a tyrant. I was ruthless and did not accept NO as a response. Why did other mothers not have this with their children? Why was I the only one? I felt trapped and alone, nobody understood. I became obsessed with my daughter not being another statistic, questioning everything, researching every possible medical procedure, ensuring she was included in every-thing she wanted to do. I also practised what I preached – 'No' or 'can't' was not a response I accepted and equally I never said these words to my daughter. She enrolled in ballet classes, acting school, did TV work, appeared in a sitcom, did live children's TV, appeared in numerous campaigns, including Red Nose Day. I firmly believed that my daughter was not another statistic, and nobody would tell me otherwise.

I was ruthless, yet this was a mask for the pain and guilt I was feeling inside. At work, I hid behind my manage-ment role. I created a label and used this to propel me forward. I was confident, competent and fully in control. I got the job done. I was good at that.

"Getting the job done" was my mantra personally and professionally. When the doctor originally told me of the diagnosis – it was just that, telling me in a way that resembled describing what she ate for lunch – in a matter-of-fact manner, I sat there stunned. All I could do was stare at my baby and cry. With no information given, other than being told I'd receive a physio appointment, I walked out of the doctor's office in a daze, with her words going around in my head. Little did I know this was the beginning of a journey that shaped the life I lead today and led me to doing things my way.

Often, I would sit in at one of the numerous hospital appointments, listening to health professionals tell me what's best for my child; allowing them to make decisions that would impact her later in life. The terminology used felt overwhelming. Just comprehending what the words meant, let alone what that meant for my daughter, was a different language. I sat and allowed this to happen because the medics knew best, right?

I worked for the same NHS Trust that my daughter received therapy from and sometimes the lines were blurred between being a mother and my professional role in the therapist's eyes. I remember on one occasion, calling a therapist as she was booked on a training course and she was very annoyed a mother would be calling her on her mobile. I reminded her I was calling in my professional role, as a manager about her training. She quickly apologised. Work was my escapism, away from caring responsibilities. I was good at my job, yet here I was, being judged on what was acceptable in the therapist's eyes and only being viewed a parent - as less worthy of her time.

The balance of living in an able bodied and disabled world was difficult to manage, yet somehow the two merged into one over time. I had lost who I was, my identity, conforming to what was expected of me, while deep down, I was hurting dreadfully. I covered it well. At work I would often go to the ladies, go into a cubicle, lock the door and cry. It was the only time I was on my own. It was all too much. The self-talk was damaging. I took the role of a victim. I was consumed with guilt; if only I had delivered her on the due date, she would not be disabled. I blamed myself. My head felt it was going to explode. I was trapped in my head with my thoughts believing everything was true. It was me against the rest of the world. At home I would disappear and sit in my bedroom alone, convinced I was of no use to anyone. Hours would go by; I didn't want to talk or eat. Sometimes I would stay fully clothed, curled in bed. My bedroom became my prison. My house became alien to me and life as a family was non-existent. But as far as the outside world was concerned, I was in control. When I felt the pressure build, I'd repeat the same story; see my GP, tell him I cried all the time. I would never admit I was not coping and ask for help. I kept quiet. I didn't know what I expected from my GP, but one thing was consistent, he would always sign me off sick with stress and depression. At the time it was a relief, but it also reinforced the way I was feeling. No other support was given and after a few weeks, I returned to work. I kept the depression quiet; nobody knew.

Working in various NHS organisations allowed me to bring my experience and knowledge in my field, something I had crafted over many years. Developing teams and working with managers was my speciality, and I was often called upon by leaders to address team dynamics or provide coaching supporting manager and leaders. I took great pleasure in seeing the transformation and the feedback was equally flattering. Many said they had never experienced such development. Others had seen dramatic service improvements. Managers and leaders felt confident and empowered in their roles as a result of our coaching sessions. I had always worked autonomously, pushed against the status quo and had a different approach to others. It was how I worked. I gave my all every time, taking pride in my work and feeling proud of making a difference. Giving value every time was standard; they succeed, I succeed was my view. I was confident in what I did and achieved results fast. I understood what managers and leaders were experiencing.

Yet, over time, things changed, I was no longer in the mix of everything and was excluded from being involved because a direct colleague and my direct manager didn't like my approach. 'It's not how we do things round here', I was told. I didn't understand the resentment. She felt I had invaded her position of being the only person responsible for training, development and coaching. The truth was, we shared the responsibilities, yet my approach was different. In their quest to undermine me, I was forbidden to speak to anyone seeking development or coaching as my colleague was territorial and this was her domain. I was instructed when running a training course to follow the exact outline and not change anything, despite knowing the content was not fit for purpose. I challenged this and was ignored. There were no discussions. I felt cast aside. I had so much to give and contribute yet I was kept down, kept in the shadows. This was evident at one of the training courses I ran and was asked if I was an external consultant as they had never heard my name. This came as a shock, and when I investigated further, I discovered my name was not included within my department.

I began to question my abilities, my competency in what I had to offer. Was I really any good at what I did? Did I really achieve a high success rate? I questioned everything about my existence. My confidence and self-belief hit an all-time low. Health suffered; symptoms were ignored when I aired how I felt. Yet despite this, and resorting to generating my own work, I returned to my pattern of coping, hiding behind a persona of confidence and smiles. I had a resilience that came from deep inside, yet I was hurting. I would hear from the managers I was coaching how unsupported they felt from their own managers and feeling bullied. Ever the professional, I did my job, never sharing how I was feeling, but it was happening to me too. Little did I know then at what cost.

Yet, it was the environment that was toxic and the culture that allowed this behaviour to continue. I had to get out of my head and not allow this to continue. I had a choice to make.

Over the years, the toll of bringing up a child with a disability was evident. The constant battles with health professionals, school and anything involving her disability was a daily occurrence. Everyone had decided what her limits were from a very early age and were reluctant to explore any alternative interventions. As far as they were concerned, having been labelled with Cerebral Palsy, there was no hope to lead an independent and successful life. We were ticking a box; their box, not mine. The NHS has a standard format clinical protocol in its treatment plan, but it wasn't enough. I was constantly being bombarded with negative comments about accepting things as they were and there was nothing else available. I didn't accept this. I was on a mission. Her consultant reviewed her progress on a yearly basis, I'd raise questions to explore other options and the reply was either let's review next year or suggest repeating a procedure that did not work previously. Waiting months to be seen to be measured for orthotics and waiting months again before fitting, meant the procedure could take six months, from start to finish. Meanwhile my daughters' feet had grown, so the orthotics were not fit for purpose. Being told we didn't qualify for school transport, because my daughter only had one disability, meant I had to continue the school runs myself, morning and afternoon in high school, while still working, plus attend all the hospital appointment, meetings, physiotherapy, orthotics and anything else that came my way.

I was doing everything for my daughter to create experiences she will remember forever and creating a belief anything was possible. Yet she was surrounded by negativity, from the people who are there to support and provide care. As her mother, I emphasised all the incredible things she was doing; surely this would change their perception of their stereotypical views? But alas, this fell on deaf ears. Ignored, as per usual. I wanted my daughter to be seen as a child first, not a girl with a disability who was unable to do anything.

When she was just two years old, and while in a physio group session with other mums, I was introduced to a therapy called Conductive Education, originating from Hungary. There was a centre in London specialising in this and their therapists (conductors) were all from the main centre in Hungary. It wasn't long before we were flying to the main centre in Hungary and spending 2-3 months a year there. We did this for six years. The NHS did not agree with this at the time, but I was seeing an improvement. My daughter was taking independent steps. Our home was filled with equipment so we could replicate the Hungarian programme. We were determined to do whatever it took to give her the best possible chance of success.

Yet we were always fighting against growth spurts and of course, the spasticity. As she was getting older, her body tired more quickly. She was starting high school soon and the physio had been encouraging me for years to book my daughter in to be measured for a wheelchair. I had resisted for so long, yet I had to put my feelings to one side and think of my daughter. I could hear the physio saying 'she'll be more independent' – this was not what I had in mind when I thought of independence. A piece of me died that day, seeing my daughter in her new wheelchair, smiling, asking me if I liked it. 'Of course,', I said, lying and holding back the tears.

It was a Monday morning and I woke up with the usual 6am alarm. With the thought of my working day ahead. I pulled back the duvet and got out of bed. As I stood and started walking, I veered to the right and walked straight into my wardrobe. Correcting myself I started walking again, grabbed the door to open it... and walked into the wall. I dismissed it thinking I was hungry and started to walk down the stairs, but I couldn't. I was unable to walk in a straight line. My arm was tingling, and I was feeling disoriented. I didn't know what was happening – I was scared. I called out for my husband to help and he sat me down on the sofa. Within minutes he was speaking with a GP who requested he bring me to the surgery. On arrival I was asked to go to a consultation room where the GP was waiting. He assured me he had spoken with a colleague because he had original suspected a heart attack. Thankfully this was not the case, but he could not give us a conclusive diagnosis. He sent me to see a specialist and following further tests, I was diagnosed with BPPV and Vestibular disorder.

This felt like déjà vu. Another diagnosis I knew nothing about, only this time the consultant was very knowledgeable and reassured me that it was treatable with specialist physiotherapy. The appointment was booked within weeks, with a treatment plan to follow.

Did I miss the signs? Could I have prevented the frightening experience of that morning, if I had noticed more things about myself? Nobody had the answers. The truth was, I had been ignoring most things when it came to my own wellbeing; putting up a persona and keeping everything hidden. There were so many more important things to focus on, so I thought in my head. Little did I know, my body was sending me signs to stop and listen. My condition did not disappear as originally told and I believe the root cause of this was the stress and internal conflict I placed myself under for years without listening to my body or looking after myself. I knew this to be true because stress and tiredness were the triggers whenever symptoms reappeared.

At work, I requested reasonable adjustments as per my physio's request and treatment plan. It was a year before anything was done. Even with a diagnosis, I was not believed as they had never heard of these conditions. I was travelling on trains across London, which I could not cope with anymore, yet I was expected to go to a London base, sit in a room on my own without speaking to anyone all day, once a week because I was told I had to be visible. In reality, I felt the opposite – invisible.

I was compromising my health, not only being excluded, but treated in a way that disrespected my professional experience and myself as a human being. Yet, there were so many managers who still needed support, and helping them helped me forget about my own issues and focused on their needs. It was a distraction.

I had been on a downward spiral for years; I felt that every part of me was damaged: mentally, emotionally and physically. Enough was enough. Looking in the mirror, I didn't recognise the person staring back at me – tired, unhappy and with the worries of the world on her shoulders. I had so many questions to ask her – Who was she? What was she doing? Where was she going with her life? One thing I was sure of was that I didn't want to continue down this path. I was exhausted, being suffocated by all these layers. I knew I wanted to be different – I wanted to be free.

It was time for me to be my own coach and seek help from others. I worked on my inner self, mindset and emotions applying everything I knew into practice. I found growth through adversity and surrounded myself with people who are mentors, coaches and a network of likeminded individuals. Having already qualified as a Master NLP Practitioner, I decided to qualify as a Health Coach. This was the foundation to really understand and know what I wanted. I knew I wanted to help women to reclaim their own identity as a result of circumstances they found themselves in, be it as managers or mothers raising children with disabilities, who needed help to rediscover who they are without hiding behind labels. I also knew I wanted to change the interaction medics had with parents, empowering and supporting them instead of talking at them in a derogatory way.

I took control of my Vestibular disorder finding a holistic way to manage the condition. Incorporating running into my weekly exercise schedule and introducing a morning regime of meditation and gratitude journaling.

The quest to find interventions to help with my daughter's disability continued. I knew a long time ago that the NHS would not have any new options – we had exhausted everything that was offered, but I knew there must be something else out there. I vowed the moment we were told of her disability; I would do everything in my power to ensure she would lead a fulfilled and independent life. I became an expert in the medical terminology and would question everything they said. When the school laughed at her dream of going to university ("It's not for people like you" they said to her," lower your expectations and have a plan B") I was shocked. I knew what she was capable of and that was certainly not meeting the school's expectations. There was one plan and that was plan A.

We were visiting friends on a Saturday afternoon and in conversation, they mentioned having just returned from the USA as they had taken their son, who was much younger, to St Louis for a life-changing operation – spinal surgery. As she was talking and explaining what this operation was, all I was thinking was 'this is it, this is what I've been searching for'. My mind was racing. I wanted this operation, but my daughter was 13 years old and ultimately it was her decision. We would support her either way.

Despite all the negative comments from the NHS, we researched the procedure and the surgeon in fine detail. What we found was, at the time, the surgeon had pioneered this surgery and had 25 years' experience performing this procedure on people - from children aged two, to adults in their 50s. Neurosurgeons were starting to travel to St Louis and observe the surgeon perform the procedure. At the time, no UK neurosurgeon was performing this procedure. How did I not know this existed? Why did the consultant fail to tell us so we could make an informed decision? All I kept thinking about was all the years of operations, orthotics, travelling to Hungary and now, aged 13, permanently in a wheelchair. If only I knew about this when she was aged two, she wouldn't have gone through everything. She would have had a normal childhood. I questioned the consultant about whether he had heard of this procedure. To my shock, he had; yet he failed to share this with me in all the years of the annual review. I was upset more so, that they clearly did not feel I, as a parent, was worthy of the discussion. That was not important, our focus now was to have an assessment to establish if my daughter is a suitable candidate.

In six months from starting the process, we had a surgery date, had raised £75,000 and had a clear prognosis post operation, quashing any early year's life predictions. I knew I was the instigator and the driving force in investigating anything new. The thought of not pursing this was not an option

For as long as I could remember, I had been focusing on what was missing - what I didn't want as opposed to want I wanted, not fully appreciating what disability has given, as opposed to what it has taken away.

Throughout my personal and professional journey, I am truly grateful for everything, especially the challenges – I would not be the person I am today without them. I discovered that removing the things I had no control over allowed my energy to focus on what was important. I couldn't change the environment I worked in, yet I had a choice how I reacted and who I was being. You see, I no longer allowed the toxic behaviour of others to impact who I was. I crafted my career and developed myself through my own means, by knowing what I wanted to achieve. I stuck to my lane regardless of other's judgments.

I had been running my business in parallel to being employed and always knew one day I would leave, yet because I loved what I did, I compromised on my happiness and health. Just as my body gave me a sign to stop and listen when diagnosed with BPPV & Vestibular, the universe decided enough was enough and I was made redundant. The message was loud and clear, it was as if the universe was reaffirming my self-belief and knew the toxic environment was holding me back and not allowing me to be me. The chameleon was gone.

You see when you declutter your environment and the people you spend time with – the battery drainers, you allow new possibilities in. Your time is spent on the things that are important and your energy is focused on what you want. You are aligned with who you are. You have clarity and are not looking for other's approval. Of course, there are times when I am faced with negativity, yet when it strikes, I'm not spending time in my head, worrying and blaming others. I deal with the facts and find a solution – is it something in my control or influence? If not, I let it go. Changing your mindset is vital, it gives you a different perception.

Doing things and thinking the way you always have will get you the same results. Connecting your heart and mind, so you are actively tuning in to your true desires, is key. If you're thinking you must do something, but your heart is not feeling the emotion that it's the right thing to do, you'll never commit to making the change. So, connect to your heart to condition the empowering emotion, while equally conditioning your mind to look for solutions not problems – glass half full, not half empty. Filter outside influences; what you allow to enter your mind does have an impact, so be mindful of what you allow in, how you respond, who you're influence by and who you listen too. Always stand guard at the door of your mind.

Some would consider I had an underdog mentality, yet I didn't live up to that title, despite other's opinions, because I had a strong belief that I was meant for more. I had a deep desire to live my purpose, what I was designed to do. My passion and mission are to ensure women facing adversity stop sabotaging their own needs and reclaim their identity to live the life they have always longed for, especially those raising children with disabilities. I stepped into my own power and used this to propel me forward into new experiences. I became a speaker, interviewed on a TV chat show, appeared in various media publications and became a published author twice, yet there is so much more I plan to do.

I'm a fully confessed self-care advocate and firmly believe your mental, physical and emotional wellbeing is non-negotiable. Every day, I feed my mind, and of course feed my body. What you eat is just as important as how you eat, as this impacts your wellbeing. Having a morning ritual saved my life – meditation, gratitude and exercise, supports my mental, physical and emotional wellbeing.

The vision and expectation I had for my daughter was clear, despite being constantly bombarded with negative comments. As far as I was concerned this was their belief, not mine, therefore it was not important. I knew I was determined to find an alternative treatment as doing nothing and watching her deteriorate was not an option.

After raising £75,000 in six months, we were in St Louis, Missouri, USA for a life-changing operation – Selective Dorsal Rhizotomy. After two months of rehabilitation, it truly was a life-changing experience. For the first time, my daughter walked onto the aero plane, something she had never experienced. It was incredible. The UK medical professionals predicted she'd never walk and would be confined to a wheelchair for life, yet here she was, walking. They were astonished at the difference.

My daughter's determination continued and she became mentally and physically stronger. This time, she was not only defying the medical professional, but also her teachers at school - especially the ones who said to not have high expectations and in sixth form, said my daughter was lucky to have a place. There was no luck involved. My daughter was very clear on what she wanted to do and stuck to her lane. She has a resilience that shines through, despite the challenges faced and comments from teachers who should know better than to put forward their limiting beliefs.

Achieving three distinction stars in sixth form, she was accepted at several universities. Last year, she graduated with a Law degree from Canterbury University and is currently studying for her Masters in International Law.

The only limitations are the ones we place on ourselves, even if they originated from others. We choose if we believe this to be true or not.

I have taken my knowledge and the experience I've gained personally and professionally to not only change my life, but also change the lives of women across the globe, leaders, managers and services in the NHS.

One of my clients came to me believing she had no confidence, lacked self-belief and continued to self-sabotage herself. My client wanted to have a career, something she had always wanted yet lacked the confidence to pursue, blaming her past and convinced she was not worthy or capable of achieving this because she listened to others. After just three coaching sessions, she is unstoppable and has secured an interview in her dream job.

Another client had anxiety and was ridiculed by members of her family. She was unhealthy, unhappy and had no self-worth or hope things would improve. After a few coaching sessions, her eating habits have improved. She is healthy, happy and now controls her anxiety. She is in control of her life and has seen a vast improvement in herself.

I was involved in an NHS Steering Group that resulted in Selective Dorsal Rhizotomy, the operation my daughter had in America, being approved as an NHS commissioned surgical procedure for children aged 3-9 with Cerebral Palsy in the UK. This was a huge step forward for the NHS and will change the lives of many children and their families.

Another client, who was in a leadership role in the NHS, came to see me as she felt stuck in her current role and felt the lack of transparency that surrounded the department she worked in. She questioned want she actually wanted to do. After several coaching sessions, she was clear about her identity. She had not known who she was as she was so consumed fulfilling her role. Plus, she now knew her values, what was important to her in her career.

During my NHS career as a training & development specialist, and having been a service user, I was fortunate to see both sides. When I was asked to provide coaching training to Speech & Language Therapists, it was a perfect way to change the way clinicians interact with parents. The results provided a change to the usual clinician led appointment, with higher engagement from parents as they felt empowered and included in their child development, and concise appointments, resulting in no duplication. This model has proved so successful with the 200 therapists trained so far, that the plan is to roll it out to all early year's therapists working with parents.

Your past does not determine your future, so stop living there. The habits and beliefs inherited do not reflect your truth today and are changed in a moment – if you choose to change them. Taking responsibility for your growth and change is down to you, not your circumstances, therefore stop blaming others. It starts with you.

Your dreams and desires are yours; no one has the right to question you. By changing our mindset, we change our perception. The question is "Who are you and what do you want out of life?"

I believe we all have a purpose. To live our dream life and be our true authentic self. Unapologetically.

Self-doubt kills any dreams.

If you are currently not where you want to be and know you are meant for more, I promise I will ignite the fire within and help you achieve this, even if you think it is not possible and doubt yourself. We will uncover your 'why' – the real reason for change.

Imagine your life a year from now; will it be the same as now? Or do you have a vision and dream of what life will look like?

If you are a woman facing adversity and who has lost her sense of identity, desperately wanting to look in the mirror and recognise herself again, love herself again… lets chat.

Is this going to be One Day or is this Day One?

ABOUT THE AUTHOR
SERA JOHNSTON

Sera Johnston is a Mindset & Health Coach and Development Consultant who helps women across the globe to thrive, reclaim their authentic self beyond motherhood, and find their own identity as women. In parallel, she works to improve communication between clinicians and parents and was named among the top 10 inspiring woman in 2020.

Before starting a business, Sera had a successful 25-year training and development career, working in management and training/coaching/facilitation positions within the NHS and the private sector. Sera now uses her skills and experience to support and empower parents of children with disabilities to live the life they've always longed for, and to change the culture and language used by organisations/health professionals, in addition to providing coaching supervision to qualified coaches

Sera loves interior design and creating mood boards before decorating a room. Sera also enjoys and regularly creates a weekly spa day at home.

Sera's available for training, coaching and development projects for organisations and individuals as well as private consultations and expert comment.

Sera has official recognition as an Accredited Provider with the CPD Standards Office.

You can reach Sera at:

Email: sera@serajohnston.com

Website: www.serajohnston.com

Facebook: https://www.facebook.com/pg/serajohnston.coachinganddevelopment/posts/

 instagram.com/serajohnston

SIMON KOZLOWSKI

PERMISSION TO RISE TO ROCKSTAR
STATUS

My clients call me the *Rockstar Marketing Guy.*

These ambitious CEO-types call on me when changing markets have forced them to reinvent their value offering, or when they want to repackage their existing products and services for new markets.

At the time of this writing, our little agency (*Marketing that ROCKS*) is less than a year old, so any success we've had should be presented with caution and humility…

BUT OUR MENTAL MODEL FOR CREATING VALUE CAN BE MORE BOLDLY ASSERTED.

Forged over 20 years, it's the fundamental framework for how we create value in and through our business.

And yet, I've never heard anyone teach this before - certainly not the way we use it.

If you're a CEO who is looking to establish your company as the preeminent *Rockstar* of your industry, then the hard-earned wisdom I share in this chapter will help you think about competitive advantage in a new and productive way.

To be sure, not everyone is an ambitious empire-builder who wants to dominate an entire industry. So, I've tried to package the insights in a way that makes sense to - and can be applied by - pretty much anyone who reads it.

To do that, I have used stories from my own working life as a metaphor for where and how businesses so often get stuck, and how they might get unstuck.

If you're a freelancer or a side-hustling employee who just wants to crank your income up by a few notches, this chapter will help you get from where you are to where you want to be, in less time, with less effort......certainly less time and effort than it took me to figure it all out.

At the *not-so-tender* age of 42, I've finally found my groove.

But on the way to figuring out what I want to do with my life, I took a lot of detours.

Over the past 24 years of my working life, I've had more than 20 jobs.

I've also had a handful of businesses.

When I look back over my life, I see that all these past jobs and businesses fall into one of three categories:

The first category is **The Labourer**.

The second category is **The Coordinator**.

The third category is **The Creator**.

These categories apply to people, but they also apply to companies.

In as far as the exchange of value is concerned, people and businesses are alike.

There is a fourth category you should know about:

The *Rockstar*.

Becoming a *Rockstar* requires a rise through the ranks of the **Labourer. Coordinator and Creator** categories … and just like artists in the music industry, **only 1 in 500,000 businesses will ever rise to this level.**

You cannot skip any of these categories, but there is a way to move through them faster than everyone else around you.

To help you rise through the levels in your business or career, let's examine the landscape of each category - the obligations, the opportunities and the obstacles.

Let's dig into **The Labourer** first, before moving onto *Coordinators* and *Creator*

The Labourer

What I call *labour* doesn't have to be physically strenuous.

It's any uninspired work that has low social value.

Labourers are easily replaced, so they typically don't get paid much.

Example:

As one of my first jobs out of school, I worked as a general assistant at a long-distance trucking company. My working hours were 7am to 7pm, from Monday to Sunday... but I did get every third weekend off.

I spent my long days processing documents ... filing documents ... stamping documents ... delivering documents ... collecting documents ... checking documents...

The truth is, I'm actually terrible at paperwork.

I really had no business doing a job like that.

The long stretches of meaningless work sucked the life out of me.

It was also an extremely toxic working environment.

One time, in a fit of drunken rage, a coworker grabbed my keyboard and started assaulting me with it … this was not a one-off event.

Despite my friends and family urging me to quit, I stayed in that job for 2 long years.

It's not because the pay was good either.

I was earning the equivalent of $200 per month, back in 1998. But I clung to that *Labourer* job for a few reasons.

They're the same reasons I ended up in other works of labour.

They're also the same reasons I failed in some *Coordinator* and *Creator* jobs and these reasons will become clearer later in the chapter.

If you're an aspiring *Rockstar*, and you find yourself doing uninspired work that has low social value, you probably want to get out of there as fast as possible.

That's a good thing.

But being a Labourer is a very important part of your journey to becoming a *Rockstar*.

So, before you attempt to rush up the ranks and become a *Coordinator*, it might help to understand how your time as a *Labourer* ultimately serves your *Rockstar* ambitions:

Being a Labourer is a time of discovery and development.

You gather information on who you are and what you bring to the world.

You figure out what works for you and what doesn't.

You get to convert your talent into skill, and turn your passion into experience.

You will be introduced to new people, perspectives and possibilities.

Sadly, I missed the memo on this.

I wasted too much time and energy being a *Labourer* for too long.

To help you avoid that unnecessary pain, allow me to share THREE ways to get the most out of your season as a Labourer:

(Translation: this is what I would do, if I had the opportunity to do it all over again).

#1. Do work that you're interested in ... even passionate about.

Back in 2002, I landed my bum in a pretty amazing job.

I was well paid (which included a nice car) to service and repair sophisticated blood analysis machines, in hospitals all over the country.

It was an intellectually challenging job, requiring a broad understanding of electronics, mechanics, chemistry and hematology (the study of blood).

I had none of the above ... and I had very little interest in any of them.

I did, however, have an interest in providing for my new family, so I gave it my all.

But working in a job (or in my case, an entire medical industry) for which I had close to zero enthusiasm, didn't energize me ... neither did all the paperwork.

If you don't already know it, energy is the whole game.

As a *Labourer*, doing energizing work will ensure that you:

➤ Power your way through steep learning curves (there will be a few);

➤ Leap over all kinds of obstacles (there will be a lot of those); and

➤ Enjoy mental and emotional rewards when there is little money or social recognition on offer (because sometimes you have to start at the bottom).

#2. Stay in your zone(s) of advantage.

In 2010, South Africa (where I live) hosted the Soccer World Cup.

I wanted to be a part of that historic event, so I took any job I could get.

That job was a Data Supervisor.

I was responsible for coordinating the 250 coaches (fancy buses with toilets) to transport 5,000+ hospitality guests to and from 25 different hotels, across 5 cities, on different match days.

That level of data management quickly overwhelmed me.

I made a ton of mistakes; needed excessive support; and was focused on my weaknesses and shortcomings.

It felt like I was working 50 times harder than everyone around me, and because that was all that I had going for me in that role, I paraded it around like a badge of honour (akin to a Purple Heart or an OBE).

But on the odd occasion, I was asked to step up and resolve a guest communication problem or negotiate a significant favour with a hotel.

In those moments, my interpersonal skills would have me shining brightly.

I was affirmed and applauded… and then the moment would be over, and I would have to return to the living hell of being a data dude.

Don't be fooled. Where attention goes, energy flows - and my efforts to fix my weaknesses under pressure produced a dismal return.

PLAYING TO YOUR STRENGTHS EFFORTLESSLY RAISES YOUR PERCEIVED VALUE.

It distinguishes you from everyone around you, builds trust and leads to more opportunities to do the same elsewhere.

This is as true for organisations as much as it is for individuals.

Confining your value offering to your zone of distinctive advantage is like an express elevator ride up into *The Coordinator* category.

#3. Understand the bigger picture.

It is possible that you can be doing work that you're interested in, and staying within your zone of advantage, and still stay stuck in *The Labourer* category.

This third way of getting the most out of your season as a labourer is also essential to moving up the ranks and becoming a *Coordinator*.

In late 2009, I had been working for a Temporary Employment Service. I had quickly risen to being (the only) national account manager, looking after a list of blue-chip clients that included the likes of *Nestle* and *Unilever* - and I'd done a pretty great job of improving efficiencies, and reducing my clients' overtime bill.

I remember approaching my General Manager about a raise - as one does when they're looking to catch up with the ballooning costs of putting three children through the education system with clothes on.

My boss opened up a super-detailed spreadsheet to reveal that my pay was disproportionately higher than that of my colleagues, while my countrywide travel resulted in a significantly higher overhead.

To make matters worse, my obsession with improved efficiency had jeopardized my chances of getting an increase - because the company made more margin when our employees worked overtime.

Whether you're a big business executive or a free-wheeling freelancer, there are a couple lessons on offer here:

1. Terms like *performance*, *value* and *Return on*

Investment are highly subjective, and extra communication is required to ensure that everyone is singing from the same balance sheet; and

2. How diligently or efficiently you work is NOT directly proportionate to the value you are expected to deliver.

Here's a quick recap on the THREE ways to get the most out of your season as a Labourer:

#1. Do work that you're interested in ... even passionate about.

#2. Stay in your zone(s) of advantage.

#3. Understand the bigger picture

When you graduate from being a *Labourer*, you rise to the level of *Connector*.

This is the category in which most professionals, coaches and consultants, salespeople, managers and executives, traders and agents operate.

It's also where the majority of sustainable and profitable companies operate.

Connectors move existing capital from one place or person to another.

To be sure, capital is not only money.

People, information and natural resources are also capital.

I'm not going to spend too much time talking about *Connectors*, but I do want to highlight a common challenge within the *Connector* category:

Because you're transferring existing capital, it can be challenging to differentiate yourself as a preferred value provider, and it's most challenging in crowded and competitive markets.

Consider these LinkedIn search results:

77,000 accountants in Sydney.

60,000 Real Estate Agents in New York.

58,000 Business Coaches in London.

And if you're a 'Digital Marketer', how do you differentiate yourself from the other 618,000 people in the world, who also have that in their LinkedIn bio?

That question nagged at my partner and I when founding Marketing that ROCKS.

But I'm getting ahead of myself here...

Whether you're a CEO who is looking to establish your company as the revered *Rockstar* of your industry, or you're a freelancer who wants to add an extra zero to your income, the way forward is the same:

Shift from deploying existing assets, to developing new assets.

In other words, go from redistributing value to reinventing value.

This is the transition from *Connector* to *Creator*.

I remember when I was forced to make this transition under extreme pressure, or risk blowing a valuable deal and incurring significant reputational damage.

In 2017, I negotiated a deal where I would co-facilitate a 4-day Digital Transformation workshop for senior government officials in a Middle Eastern nation, on behalf of a UK based training company.

In the lead up to the event, my Dutch co-facilitator and I spent three weeks diligently stitching together what (to our minds) was an amazing innovation program.

The client's invoice for this 4-day workshop was around £260,000.

Keep in mind that at this point, no new value had been created.

All of the intellectual, social and financial value had merely been transferred from different people and places into this workshop.

The event kicked off with much pomp and parade, and Arabian royalty arrived to inaugurate the event with speeches that (almost) made the workshop sound like the most important event since that nation's founding.

But the hype was short-lived.

Early on the second day, a few attendees approached us to report that dissatisfied murmurings were rippling through the group. Those murmurings built throughout the day, and ultimately crescendoed in a late afternoon meeting with senior leaders.

The programme we were delivering was not meeting their expectations.

Those expectations appeared to be based on the glossy 5-page brochure that had been produced for the event - more specifically, they were based on a short parenthetical list on the bottom left corner of page 3.

This disconnect between expectation and experience is not uncommon.

As *industry experts*, we make assumptions about what the market wants and needs.

Those assumptions are usually immersed in the status quo - existing competitor offerings, historical market patterns, and accepted industry norms.

When we attempt to create value based on "what we already know to be true", market research becomes an echo chamber that produces more of the same.

But value is determined by the market.

Markets are continuously shifting and evolving.

So too are the market expectations and experiences.

Without clarity on what the end customer wanted, we had created a Digital Transformation workshop based on "what we already knew to be true".

We were confident that we had created something amazing.

Our delegates had weighed the workshop against their expectations of value, and plunged a dagger of discontentment into the heart of that confidence.

We weren't about to make that mistake a second time.

As innovation consultants, we already knew the theory of effective value creation:

Those businesses and brands that disrupt and dominate their markets are the ones who can align their value creation efforts with the UNFILTERED expectations and desired experiences of their ideal customers.

This is in stark contrast to the traditional approach of surveying the market; filtering that feedback through internal 'expert' committees; and then adapting value creation efforts for optimum internal compliance and convenience.

We had fallen into this trap.

We weren't about to make the same mistake twice.

That evening, having acquired the email addresses and telephone numbers of all the delegates, we sent out a questionnaire (endorsed by a senior government official, with a 'request' for urgent response).

We worked through the night to create a new Digital Transformation workshop that addressed every delegate's specific interests, questions and concerns.

As an added touch of personalization, we made sure to reference the delegate feedback at every point of the facilitation over the next two days, acknowledging each person by name for their contribution to improving the programme.

Admittedly, the tide of discontentment took a few hours to turn.

But by the end of the programme, we had managed to re-engage our audience.

(Okay, we actually received some high praise; moving along swiftly…)

As reactionary as it was, stepping out of a *Connector* role and embracing the mandate of a *Creator*, resulted in a vivid, technicolour realisation:

VALUE CREATION NEEDS MARKETING; AND MARKETING NEEDS VALUE CREATION.

When these two work in harmony, a special kind of magic happens.

It's the kind of magic that is indispensable to becoming a *Rockstar* of your industry.

I'M A FIRM BELIEVER IN DEFINING MOMENTS... I'VE HAD TOO MANY OF THOSE MOMENTS NOT TO.

One such defining moment was after that workshop, during our trip to the airport.

My Dutch colleague turned to me and said, *"Buddy, we were total Rockstars!"*

I let out a slightly-too-boisterous laugh.

I didn't *REALLY* think that I was a Rockstar, but in that moment the question stuck with me:

How does one become a Rockstar in their industry?

And so began a somewhat obsessive study of how *Rockstars* rise to prominence:

Janis Joplin ... Freddie Mercury ... Tina Turner ... Jimi Hendrix ... Joan Jett.

I plunged deep into the stories of no less than 50 music icons.

Where did they come from... how did they become so famous?

What made them so magnetic... so mesmerizing?

It certainly wasn't their elite vocational education - neither Jimi Hendrix, Elvis Presley, Eric Clapton or The Beatles could read sheet music.

I then explored celebrated Rockstars in other categories:

Walt Disney ... Oprah Winfrey ... Steve Jobs ... Sarah Blakely ... Elon Musk.

What did these business greats have in common with the icons of Rock?

How much of that could be systematized and productized?

I then compared and contrasted the most celebrated musicians with some of their contemporaries who were equally (if not more talented), but weren't able to rise to King-of-the-Category levels of success:

The Ramones ... Gene Clark ... Mark Arm ... Syd Barrett ... The Cardiacs.

One of my earliest observations was that, with a few exceptions, the *Creators* who rose to *Rockstar* status - whether in music or in business - weren't significantly more talented or skilled than their less famous contemporaries. When you adjust for all the typical factors that contribute to success, it pretty much comes down to marketing - specifically how the marketing of *Rockstars* intersected with their creation processes.

Let me be the first to say that I'm no investigative journalist.

My method of research was hardly scientific.

I just read as many books and articles as I could get my hands on, and listened to more interviews than I can remember - allowing the information to wash over me, until a theory naturally began to emerge.

Over time, my theory evolved in the *ROCKS* ideology.

ROCKS is the foundation upon which our business is built.

ROCKS is an acronym for Resonance, Originality, Continuity, Kingship & Structure.

These are the key criteria for catapulting creators into the realm of the *Rockstar*.

R is for Resonance.

Resonance is about emotional connection and impact.

It's when your mission and message strum on the heartstrings of your audience.

Resonant messaging expresses your target audience's cares and concerns, and speaks to their goals and aspirations, in their own language. It expresses your own thoughts and feelings back to you, in a way that makes you feel deeply understood.

O is for Originality.

The human brain is drawn to anything that's new, different or unusual.

The always-on information-filing machine that is our brain, already has folders and detailed files for most of the things we encounter on a daily basis - including thousands of brand and product categories.

If your ideal customer's brain already has a file for whatever it is that you're offering - and it probably does - it only takes a couple of seconds to whip out the relevant folder and file you away, so it can hurry on to the next shiny object.

Being original puts that mental filing machine in a tough situation:

It's forced to stop and pay closer attention, so that it can create a brand-new file in which to place your message and your value offering.

C is for Continuity.

Continuity is about meeting your customers at the point of their dissatisfaction, and escorting them, via your value offering, toward satisfaction.

These dissatisfactions might be financial, physical, psychological, social or emotional.

K is for Kingship.

Kingship is all about establishing your offering as the undisputed authority in your very own niche.

But not just any niche… a niche that your business designed and defined.

Category Kings (or Queens) are able to frame old problems in a new and unique way.

Those that frame the problem the best, ultimately win.

S is for Structure.

In both value creation and marketing, good structures produce great results.

When you have the right frameworks and processes, producing and promoting your value offering becomes as easy as getting a catchy tune stuck in your head.

More than just a pocket of stories and a handful of insights, I'd love for you to come away from this chapter with something that you can practically apply to your own value creation and promotion efforts, so...

Allow me to share the framework that we use at *Marketing that ROCKS*, when crafting and communicating compelling value on behalf of our clients.

Whether we're building out automated online sales funnels or composing high value corporate proposals and pitches, our general structure (the 'S' in ROCKS) is the same.

This structure ensures that our clients generate a twenty times return on their investment with us - creating value offerings that bring in revenue upwards of US$750,000.

But these same clients would insist that it's not about the money. They're often driven by a much deeper desire than mere market dominance.

They're in business for impact and legacy.

To quote Steve Jobs, our client is *"someone who really wants to make a little dent in the universe."*

We dare to suggest that our structure is up to that task.

But if you're a freelancer or a side-hustling employee who just wants to crank your income up by a few notches, this structure does a pretty fine job of that too.

We call this structure *The ROCKSTAR Framework*.

And yes, you guessed it, it's another acronym.

Here's what it looks like:

R = Resonate, Relate and Reveal.

O = Outlook, Obstacles, Outcomes and Opportunity.

C = Compound the Cost.

K = Knowledge and Key Insight.

S = Significance, Struggle and Solution.

T = Transformation and Testimonials.

A = Announcement, Appraisal & Appeal.

R = Reduce the Risk.

While our clients will pay mid 5-figure fees to have us apply this framework for them, I'm going to save you a few bucks and provide some pretty detailed instructions on how to apply it for yourself.

But first, I want to make something clear:

It's NOT impossible to use *The ROCKSTAR Framework* purely as a promotional mechanism - i.e., to skip over the important innovation and market adaptation work - and still get amazing results.

But that is not the true purpose (or best use) of the framework.

Remember what I said earlier:

VALUE CREATION NEEDS MARKETING; AND MARKETING NEEDS VALUE CREATION.

Sacrifice either one of these, and you sabotage your *Rockstar* potential.

Okay, let's dig into *The ROCKSTAR Framework*...

To make *The ROCKSTAR Framework* super easy to understand and apply, I've unpacked it below in the form of a quick-start *sales page* template - so you can pretty much fill in the blanks.

R

Resonate

If you are... **[target audience]**

Example: *a second-generation Polish immigrant in London.*

One of the greatest paradoxes of the rise to Rockstar fame, is that it begins hyper-focused.

A foundational human desire is to be heard, seen and acknowledged. When you speak directly to an over-looked and underserved segment of the market, in a language that appeals to them, you will command attention - without attention, you will never rise to Rockstar status.

Go deep on a narrow audience; it will make all the difference.

Relate

who is tired of... **[the problem that they want to overcome]**

Example: *listening to painful hold music while waiting to speak to someone at your bank.*

and wishes that... **[the future that they desire for themselves]**

Example: *there was a fast and affordable way to get six pack abs.*

Reveal

then I want to tell you about... **[benefit + category summary]**

Example: *a luxury island escape that will purge your stress and recharge your soul.*

The human brain has a very basic organising system: it identifies everything that we see and experience as either a 'threat' or a 'reward' - i.e., a pain or a desired gain. Every moment of every day, our brain is working hard to move us away from PERCEIVED Pain and toward PERCEIVED Gain.

These *Pains* and *Desired Gains* can be physical, psychological, environmental and social - and all of them culminate in a rich emotional stew that drives our decision-making.

No matter how logical you might think you are, countless brain studies show that we all make emotional choices, and then substantiate and validate those choices with 'logic'.

Don't just dig into the problem, dig into the emotions that the problem is producing.

O

Outlook

You are not the only one who... **[self-talk/psychology]**

Example: *feels unworthy and ashamed when the church collection plate is going around.*

Obstacles

Because... **[shortcoming/barrier]**

Example: *any attempts to quit drugs always seem to coincide with your most stressful days.*

In our attempts to move from *Pain* toward Gain, we run into what I call *obstacles* and *enemies that* hinder our progress - or even send us backward. **Obstacles** are external, and include: Environmental, Social and Financial barriers. **Enemies** are internal, and include: Physical, Psychological and Emotional opposition.

Our job as both value creators and marketers, is to come alongside our customer, and help them to overcome their *obstacles* and conquer their *enemies.*

Outcomes

Which leaves you... **[perceptions & judgements]**

Example: *feeling rejected and alone, because nothing you do is ever good enough for him.*

Opportunity

The good news is that you can **[desired outcome]** without **[undesirable process]**

Example: achieve the body of a Greek god without being on a diet of rabbit food.

~

C

Compound the Cost

The bad news is that **[likely outcome if the problem is not addressed]**

Example: the longer you leave your eczema untreated, the worse it gets.

~

K

Knowledge

What most experts don't tell you **[little known or shared truth]**

Example: "Cholesterol-free" can be bad for your cholesterol.

Key Insight

That's why **[the against the grain assertion]**

Example: limiting your working day to 3 hours per day makes your 5X more productive.

~

S

Significance

I'm passionate about this because [**reason for committing to solving this problem**]

Example: my father was killed by a drunken driver.

Struggle

In my own life [**briefly share personal experience**]

Example: I would always do something stupid to sabotage a perfectly good relationship.

Solution

But then [**the brief story of how the solution emerged**]

Example: I was introduced to the Presleyterian diet of bacon, Pepsi and peanut butter.

∿

T

Transformation

And now [**summary of the radical shift experienced**]

Example: my formerly flunking children now get straight A's on every test.

Testimonies

And I'm not the only one... **[how others have benefited from the solution]**

Example: my next-door neighbour, Jeff, is now getting 45 miles to the gallon.

~

A

Announce

Introducing... **[unveiling of the value offering]**

Example: Armageddon, the most powerful surface cleaner on the planet.

Appraise

Here's what you get... **[all the features, benefits and meanings]**

Example: ...and 10,000 satellite connectivity, to ensure perfect signal anywhere on earth.

Appeal (Action)

Don't wait... **[likely outcome if the problem is not addressed]**

Example: If you call today, our team will have those giant rats removed before sunset, so they don't multiply while you're sleeping.

R

Reduce the Risk

You have nothing to worry about… **[personal commitment if failure to deliver]**

Example: *if we don't double your investment, we'll pay you the difference.*

There's a lot more to unpack here, but (given the limitations of a single chapter) I hope that offers you enough insight into the framework, and how to use it to both create new value and promote that value to your target audience.

If I was to sum the framework up in a single grab-n-go statement, I would say:

R = Rationalize your customers' shortcomings,

O = Offset their anxiety,

C = Confirm their suspicions,

K = Kick their enemies in the shins, and

S = Spur them on toward their ambitions.

You might be reading this and wondering to yourself:

What proof do you have that The ROCKSTAR Framework actually works?

One of my favourite client case studies is one where two life coaches, with no experience in corporate consulting, landed a US$70,000 coaching gig with a fast-growing multinational financial company.

That deal was more than 7X what either of them had thought it could be worth.

When they approached me, *John* and *Jack* (not their real names) had very little idea how they were going to structure their offering, and to get the work, they were going to have to outdo some far more experienced companies, who had some very impressive client lists.

While some tight non-disclosure agreements prevent me from spilling all the juicy details, I can use some broad strokes (and an oversized brush) to illustrate how we used The ROCKSTAR Framework to create and communicate a too-good-to-refuse value offering:

(R) Resonate + Relate + Reveal

We took the time to understand who the internal decision-makers and influencers were, and what each of their respective objectives, goals and concerns were - and to be sure, they were not in alignment.

We proposed a big idea that pulled all these agendas into a big, happy, group hug.

(O)
Outlook+Obstacles+Outcomes+Opportunity

(C) Compound the Cost

We highlighted the *"surprising internal challenges"* that our research had revealed, and presented (widely available) data on how similar organisations who had failed to intelligently address those problems were suffering because of it.

(K) Knowledge + Key Insight

This is where the big idea came in. Originally, the brief was to propose employee coaching that could plug into a larger company-run initiative. Our proposal inverted the hierarchy, by presenting our offering as the key to the success of the overarching initiative.

(S) Significance + Struggle + Solution

(T) Transformation + Testimonials

This was a significant weakness that we needed to turn into a strength. Even the most glowing testimonials in John and Jack's arsenal were out of alignment with the value that was needing to be communicated.

To offset this, we arranged and facilitated a few free coaching sessions, in order for key decision-makers to personally experience the value on offer.

I often say that experiences are like children: You always value your own more than anyone else's.

(A) Announce + Appraise + Appeal

(R) Reduce the Risk

DO YOU WANT TO KNOW WHAT I LOVE MOST ABOUT THIS CASE STUDY?

There were actually two pricing options, with the lower option being US$55,000. But when that lower option was presented to the client, he rushed to reject it.

That wasn't a happy accident either.

That's the result of achieving harmony between your value creation and marketing.

MY PARTING SHOT

Do you want to know what REALLY sucks about this book format?

I cannot see you … I cannot hear you!

There's no way for me to click on your profile picture or read your bio.

That makes it insanely difficult to know how to best serve you.

YOU MIGHT BE STUCK IN THE *LABOURER* CATEGORY, RIGHT NOW.

Maybe your work doesn't light you up, maybe the pay stinks. If that's where you find yourself, then I want to encourage you to:

Use this time to gather information on who you are and what you bring to the world.

Try to take a step back and figure out what works for you and what doesn't.

Focus on converting your talent into skill, and turning your passion into experience.

I strongly urge you to do work that you're interested in; to figure out your zone of genius; and take time to understand the bigger picture of what's going on around you - how value is moving all around you, waiting to be harnessed by you.

MAYBE YOU'RE IN THE *CREATOR* CATEGORY.

I celebrate your extraordinary creative powers.

Thank you for manifesting your ideas and insights in the world.

Now take a moment to look within yourself...

Are you *"someone who really wants to make a little dent in the universe"*?

Yes? Then I want to invite you to embrace the calling of the *Rockstar*.

Begin by immersing yourself in *ROCKS Ideology*.

Embrace and apply *The ROCKSTAR Framework*.

Would you like support and encouragement as you rise to Rockstar status?

I'm committed to supporting *Creators* in becoming celebrated *Rockstars*.

This has become my mission and my purpose.

If you're ready to become a Rockstar-on-the-Rise...

Then check out www.marketingthat.rocks/yourwaybook

There you will find a full tour bus of *Rockstar* resources.

Finally, in the slightly mangled words of AC/DC:

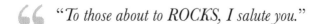 *"To those about to ROCKS, I salute you."*

ABOUT THE AUTHOR

SIMON KOZLOWSKI

Often referred to as the Rockstar Marketing Guy, Simon helps established businesses reinvent themselves for success in rapidly changing markets.

Simon spent a decade meandering through the corporate coaching and training space, before being smitten by innovation consulting. He quickly rose to prominence by simplifying the heady science of business model and product innovation, with his INVENT Model™ and Reinvention Roadmap™.

In 2018, he accepted the invitation to serve as *Business Development Director for Sub-Saharan Africa,* at a global advertising agency, where his clients included big names such as P&G, L'Oréal and Mars.

But a few months into the global shutdowns of 2020, Simon saw a way to bring the worlds of advertising and innovation together in a way that enables businesses to pivot and prosper - and so, *Marketing that ROCKS* was born.

When he's not dreaming about business and marketing ideas, Simon can be found immersing himself in culinary adventures with his wife, and making hollow promises about getting back into surfing someday.

If you're looking to reinvent or repackage your existing product/service for new or changing markets, you can reach him at simon@marketingthat.rocks, or look him up and connect on LinkedIn.

PERSONAL NOTE OF CONGRATULATIONS

Being part of this journey with these authors has been nothing short of incredible, each one of them has taken action and grown in ways we never considered possible before.

We always knew they were an incredibly special group of individuals when we initially welcomed them into Sell Your Way ™ and they certainly have been.

It's been an honour for us to share this time, space and experience with them. To be trusted by them in their wobbles, to hold their hand when they needed extra support and be with them to celebrate their wins, highs and transformations.

It isn't easy deciding to blaze your own path, to choose to do it your way but non the less they committed to doing just that. It also isn't necessarily easy going on a journey of self discovery, taking action on things you'd previously talked yourself out of doing or going through this process of writing a book. But they did it!

So this is a message to all of you incredible authors, thank you and we celebrate you more than you could ever know.

We celebrate all you for saying yes to this journey.

For all of the growth.

For all of the breakthroughs.

For these chapters.

For the wins.

For deciding to do it your way!

We couldn't be prouder and we hope you're truly proud of yourselves too.

SARAH STONE

Sarah Stone is a trusted and highly sought after Holistic Strategist for Life, Business & Home. As the Founder & CEO of Creative Feng Shui®, Award Winning Entrepreneur and Best Selling Author of Live What You Love, Sarah has over two decades of experience within the personal development and holistic growth space.

Her global clients choose to work privately with Sarah in particular because she's not locked into a specific formula or rule book. Instead, she advises on a personally prescribed basis. Her vast experience and perspective working with clients in a variety of ways over the years has helped position her as an established, proven expert in her field.

One thing that allows Sarah to truly stand out is that she helps her clients look beyond the trends, jargon and template formulas. She has the intuitive and intentional ability to simplify your life, see opportunities to enhance your space and position her clients incomparably for their next level of wealth, health and success.

By harnessing the power of Creative Feng Shui® and the Five Elements Formula®, Sarah combines the ancient technique of traditional Feng Shui, strengths based practices, energetic tools, nature elements and holistic strategy to consciously create and intentionally live a limitless life filled with purpose, fulfilment, abundance & flow.

Sarah's work has been instrumental in creating a profound new way of cultivating positive change and helping to transform her clients' world with higher levels of fortune in money, success, love, relationships and every other area of their life.

She's now on a personal mission to empower others to gain a fresh perspective on their version of 'success' so that more people can truly live a life they love; without the hustle, chaos, anxiety, burnout or stress.

You can find out more about Sarah and her work at

www.sarahstone.com

 facebook.com/sarahstoneonline
 instagram.com/sarahstoneonline

JANE BAKER

Jane is, an award winning entrepreneur, featured in Forbes and listed as a top 100 UK female entrepreneur. Jane is also a multiple best selling author of She Lives Limitlessly & She Sells Effortlessly, Founder of the DISRUPT sales superpower system, Media Personality, CEO of an international group of companies, philanthropist and a high ticket sales strategist & consultant.

With over a decade of experience in the entrepreneur world Jane has blazed her way to multiple 7 figures, often turning her back on the norms expected in each industry.

Jane now focus on working with online business owners, coaches, experts and persons of influence helping them unlock their own sales super powers and through leveraging the high ticket model helps them sell 5, 6 and even 7 figure offers with ease and in total alignment whilst also unlocking time freedom so that they can live a limitless life they love.

After a few short weeks working in a call centre aged 16 and feeling as if she was useless at selling Jane is passionate about empowering others to embrace selling, to reprogramme their own relationship with sales and create something more empowering that enables them to, charge their worth and blaze their way to their version of success by utilising methods and strategies that are in complete alignment with themselves and who they're selling to.

You can find out more about Jane and her work at www.iamjanebaker.com

 facebook.com/IAmJaneBaker

 instagram.com/IAmJaneBaker

Printed in Great Britain
by Amazon